WHAT THE REVIEWERS SAY

"...a valuable resource for those building and remodeling as well as purchasing houses."

BOOKLIST

"...Ferguson asserts that the more user-friendly the design to the individual's lifestyle and/or situation, the greater the quality and value of the house, and he backs up his assertion with careful arguments...Recommended..."

LIBRARY JOURNAL

"...Written in plain language...He (Ferguson) provides hundreds of tips on design and building materials...The 15-page construction checklist is invaluable."

Chicago Sun-Times

"If you're gathering material about building a house, you might add "Build It Right!" (DIMI PRESS, $16.95) to your collection."

Detroit Free Press

"(Build It Right!) is full of detailed yet easy-to-understand information about kitchens, beds and baths, electrical and plumbing systems, windows, exteriors and more. There's also advice on how to choose a good builder. Includes photos, glossary, checklists, recommended reading."

THE ST. PETERSBURG TIMES

"Before you break ground, break open this book!...It can save you time, money, and frustration by helping you to make the right decisions ahead of time."

McGraw-Hill/TAB Book Clubs

BUILD IT RIGHT!

MYRON E. FERGUSON

DIMI PRESS

DIMI PRESS
3820 Oak Hollow Lane, SE
Salem, Oregon 97302-4774
© 1994 by Myron Ferguson. All rights reserved.

First edition, second printing

Library of Congress Cataloging-in-Publication Data

Ferguson, Myron.
       Build it right! : how to put value and quality in your new
   home / by Myron Ferguson. -- 1st ed.
          p. cm.
   Includes index.
   ISBN: 0-931625-23-8
   1. Buildings--Defects. 2. House buying. I. Title.
TH441.F47   1994
   643'.12'0979--dc20   93-31061
                                                      CIP

This book is a work of advice and opinion. Neither the author nor
the publisher is responsible for actions based on the contents of this
book.

**A selection of the Architects' Book Club, the How-To Book Club, the
Civil Engineers' Book Club, and the Better Homes and Gardens
Book Clubs**

Edited by Linda West
Layout by Debbie Wuerth
Cover design by Multnomah Graphics
Cover illustration courtesy of Alan Mascord Design Associates
Publicity by Theresa Van Winkle

FOREWORD

For many years I have been amazed at the way people buy homes. They seem to be much more interested in the cost per square foot than the qualifications of the builder of their most expensive purchase. To compare houses by the cost per square foot is like comparing a pound of sunflower seeds to a pound of T-bone steaks—the only commonality is the weight. Buyers will invest both time and money researching the most prudent car or electronics purchase, but when it comes to their single most expensive lifetime purchase, their home, emotion seems to be the decision-making tool.

They should check the qualifications and references of any potential builder. The outward appearance of the home tells them little about the builder whom they expect to stand behind the product. It is sad to see buyers lose their excitement over their new home because they are unable to communicate knowledgeably with the builder or because they find him or her unresponsive to their service requests. If they had taken the time to check out their builder with previous buyers and the appropriate construction contractors' licensing agency, they might have been able to avoid these potential problems.

Don't allow yourself to be rushed into decisions. As a builder of custom homes, I try to go over everything with the buyers. I personally do not like to deal with after-the-contract change orders. I would much rather expend more time initially to discover the wants and desires of my customers and communicate these back and forth. Of course, knowledgeable consumers make for more fruitful discussions and that makes my job easier.

Build It Right! is needed. Congratulations to Myron Ferguson for seeing that need and putting together a book to address it.

Michael Meaghers
Director, National Association of Home Builders
Past President, Oregon Home Builders Association

Author's Preface

I didn't start out to write a book, especially about houses. I've always been a home user, not a home builder.

When we moved into our new home in Oregon, we were displeased by things like light switches in the wrong places and a refrigerator that's fouled up because of the kitchen layout. Then after a few weeks I realized that there were several more things which had become irritants. My curiosity took over and that was it. I started to look at other new unsold houses to see if there were things in them that would make the ultimate buyers disgruntled. And I found that our house was among the better ones!

Before retirement I was a communications satellite system engineer since the first COMSAT satellites in the 1960s. My design ideas were incorporated into a lot of satellite systems built in the 1970s and 1980s. Surprisingly, that experience was responsible for what happened next in my house investigations. Anyone who is successful in the kind of work I did has to understand how the overall system fits into the world of telecommunications and he has to understand what each and every part of it does and why. So, when I saw these things that are not user-friendly in new homes, it was natural for me to ask, "Why?" and to be persistent in getting sensible answers.

This started a long investigation into the many facets of home building: materials, techniques, local peculiarities and prejudices, building codes, and, most importantly, the people who build houses. My first reaction was that builders are a really inept bunch who go about foisting their inferior products on a gullible public. At that point I was encouraged by a real estate broker to write a book about the things I had seen. This led to more research and, as this book is going to press, I've looked at close to 500 new houses in four states and one Canadian province.

All of this led me to a realization that builders are pretty much like the rest of us. They make what they can sell and do what they can to maximize their profits. The reason they build these short comings into houses is that everyone accepts them and the houses sell just fine. And the reason everyone accepts them is that nobody has pointed out how things can be better.

The home-building industry is a very important part of our economy. It would be beyond what one person could expect to do in a lifetime to find everything that is good and bad in new houses. And to put it all in writing would result in a library in itself. So *Build It Right!* is proffered with a large hunk of humility. I've scratched the surface and I've tried to include the most important points. I have no doubt that it can and will be a large help to buyers, designers, builders, and sellers of new houses. I've had the chance to make a survey that they haven't. And I've done it with a critical curiosity that comes from my training and experience which most people don't have.

The book is not earth shaking. I didn't invent anything, it's just reporting what I saw. There's a companion book to be published soon for people who are buying spec and tract houses. I've started Home User Advocates, a small consulting business, to help people with their new homes. And I'm looking forward to seeing the impact all of this has on making at least a few new homes more enjoyable places to live.

It is impossible to single out the literally hundreds of people who have helped me with the book. Most of them didn't realize they were doing it. In looking at all of those houses, I met the real estate agents who went with them and some of these people had very useful insights into their business. Home shows were another place where people helped, again unwittingly. Suppliers and subcontractors had inputs. And the builders themselves, some pleasant and urbane and others hard-working tradesmen, all contributed. To all of you, whether you remember me or not, thanks for putting up with my probing and my biting commentary.

To Bob McElroy a special note of appreciation for his willingness to work his way through an early draft and his encouragement to keep at it.

Three of our sons, Greg, Curt, and Chris, bought new homes while all of this was going on. Their observations and the chance to discuss things after they had lived in their homes for a while resulted in a number of the recommendations you'll find in the book.

I don't know how to put this last part. If you've never been through the pains and agonies of a first book, it would be hard to understand the stress it can put on a marriage. For your help and patience in equally huge doses, "Thank you, Jean."

Contents

Part I—The First Steps

Part II—The Whole-House Systems

Part III—The Parts of the House

Contents

Part IV—Fulfillment

Part V—Appendices and Glossary

Contents

Introduction

If you had the time and inclination to travel around the country and look at over 450 new houses and if you were observant and critical, you'd be in a position to have some very good ideas about what you want in your custom-built dream home. If you can't do that then welcome to *Build It Right!*

New homes come in two flavors, custom and tract or spec. *Build It Right!* deals with custom homes. A companion book looks at many of the same considerations for people who are buying an existing new house or a house in a tract or subdivision. For them the question is which of the available houses is best. For you the dream is different, the house isn't there when you start. You get to decide what it's to look like, what's to go in it, and who's going to build it.

A shortcoming of books on home building and buying is that they are not written from the perspective of people who will be living in the houses. They are written by builders and are about a lot of stuff they know that's of little interest to you and the books are not about a lot of stuff you should know.

Build It Right! was written to fill the gap. The book looks at a house as a place for you to live. It considers things other books ignore, things that, to borrow a couple of terms from the computer age, are ergonomic and user-friendly.

The need for a more user-oriented approach to home design and building is not confined to any single geographic region. The same good and bad features were seen in houses from border-to-border and in published floor plans in national magazines and in home designers' catalogs.

As with everything you buy, you should shop to get what's best for you. If you're like most of us, a home is very different from anything else you buy. It's by far the most expensive single item you'll ever purchase and you know very little about what makes a house a good home. To get value and quality you need to be knowledgeable. That's where *Build It Right!* comes in—it puts you in a far better position to get a home you'll enjoy while you're living in it and one that will have more value when you have to sell.

The book is in five parts:

1. The first steps: getting a lot, deciding on a house design and choosing a house designer, if you need one.

2. Considerations that involve the whole house: electrical, heating, plumbing, doors, interior finishes, windows, etc.

3. The parts of the house: room by room and area by area.

4. Fulfillment: selecting a builder and checking things as the house is being built.

5. Glossary and appendices.

You'll find examples of flaws that were seen in new houses, flaws you won't want in your own home. Every one of these exists in somebody's home today.

The book contains over fifty illustrations and photographs depicting different aspects of a home. Some show good ways to do things, others are of things you'll want to avoid.

You'll notice that finding a builder is toward the last part of the book, not at the beginning. If you decide that you want the builder to tell you what you should have in your home then read that chapter first. But if you want to make the decisions about the place **you** are going to live, then learn all you can before you make that most critical of choices, selecting a builder.

You'll appreciate the glossary—it will make life easier as you get into the unfamiliar jargon of home building. You'll notice that an unusually large portion of the book is dedicated to appendices. This comes about because of my conviction that you, the readers, should know what's behind each and every one of the recommendations and suggestions made in the book. Some of this background is very detailed. It's there, in the appendices, for you to consider as you need it or as the mood strikes you.

Use *Build It Right!* just like most how-to books. Go through it once to familiarize yourself with what's there. Then go back and re-read the sections that apply to your circumstances. Use the book to check and double check your house from the start of the design until the end of the construction.

Now it's time to get started.

Part I

The First Steps

Getting Started
Lots
House Designers
House Designs
Interior Designers

Chapter 1

Getting Started

Your Home Buying Options

After you decide to buy a new home, one of your next decisions will be whether to buy a house that has already been built (a spec house), to buy a house which is a copy of a model in a tract, or to have your dream home custom built.

Many home-owners-to-be believe that custom houses cost more than spec or tract houses. This isn't necessarily so. With a custom house, there are no real estate agent's fees to pay. Most often, the extra cost of getting a custom house is not in dollars but in your involvement in the process.

Nobody said it wasn't work.

In considering a custom house, where do you start? There are so many things that seem to need doing first: finding a lot, a house design, financing, getting a builder—the list seems endless and all are big decisions. At this point, you might be tempted to back off and buy that "ho-hum" house in the local subdivision.

You shouldn't. Getting a custom house is well within just about any one's ability. But there is work involved. You'll have to figure out just what you want, not as a nebulous dream, but as something that can be put onto paper.

One of life's greatest satisfactions can come from starting from scratch and ending up with a home that's the result of your ideas and decisions. Help is there waiting for you. New businesses are coming into being to serve you. You can even be your own general contractor! This may seem ridiculous to you right now, but it's not that difficult with the help of companies that have formed specifically to help you make decisions that general contractors make and to help you save the money that a contractor needs for overhead and profit.

The Why and How of Custom Houses

People buy custom houses for several reasons:

1. They want a truly one-of-a-kind of house.

2. They've found a special lot, usually with a great view.

3. They're in an area where there are few tracts and these are all low-priced starter homes. So it's either a spec house or a custom house and, since most builders make both, they save at least the realtor's fee if they have it custom built.

4. They want to do part of the work themselves and can work out a deal with a builder who will let them do this.

There are two ways to go about getting your custom house built:

1. Work with only one builder from the start

2. Get a set of specifications and get bids from several builders.

Most builders like to do custom houses for several reasons. First, the uncertainty associated with building a spec house and having it not sell is gone. Second, once the contract is finalized, they know what their selling price is and how much profit margin they are working with, so a large part of the risk is gone. Third, in many cases the margins are higher because they get the job without competition.

Whether you work with only one builder or go through the competitive bidding process depends in large part on how much extra money you're willing to spend to make your job simpler.

Working with One Builder

The easy way to find a builder is to visit spec houses that builders have for sale in your area. When you find a house you like, you work with the builder to select a lot and a house design, agree on a price, work up a contract, and build the house. A variation of this is to select the lot first, then get a builder.

This is the easy method insofar as you don't have to know very much about houses and you depend on the builder's expertise to guide you through the many decisions that have to be made. It's also the way to end up with a user-unfriendly house. And it can be more expensive.

Here are the risks:

1. The builder won't do his pricing in a competitive environment and will have no incentive to keep the price down.

2. The builder may not be particularly good at working with you to make the house a reflection of your needs. Such a house often reflects the builder's own likes and dislikes and not the buyer's.

3. You won't have anyone looking out for you in the process, other than you. The builder may be competent and honest, but will only do what he's told to do or what he knows.

It never hurts to get advice and help from someone else who has no ax of his own to grind. You get this when you involve an architect or designer on your side as happens when you get competitive bids.

Getting Competitive Bids

The first steps in getting competitive bids are to find a lot and to get a house design, either from a catalog or from an architect or building designer. You get a set of specifications for the house. You get bids for the house from several suitable builders and select one. You finalize the contract and work with the builder to have the house built. Depending on your arrangement with the designer, one or the other or both of you may be involved in checking that the builder follows the plans and specifications.

This approach isn't easy although it can be more rewarding. It requires that you either learn more about what goes into a house than most people do or get the advice of someone who does, preferably both. Unless you're perfectly satisfied with plans you buy from a catalog, you'll need the services of a building designer to adapt a set to your ideas. Or the designer can start with some ideas you have and develop them for you. These services are costs you don't have when you work with a single builder. On the other hand, without detailed specifications you don't have much control over what's done. The services of the designer or architect may well be paid for by a lower competitive construction cost for the house. And you're more likely to get what you want, not what the builder happens to give you.

Your Responsibilities

The amount of responsibility you are willing to take will determine how close the house comes to being the dream you started out to get. If you take the time to understand what your options are and to get the ones you want into the contract you have with the builder, you're going to be much better off than the person who doesn't. The more you leave up to the builder, at least with regard to the things that make a house friendly, the more likely you are to find user-unfriendly things when you move in. And unless you want the process to drag on and on, you must be prepared to make many decisions in a relatively short period of time. The better prepared you are by having done your homework ahead of time, the better the results will be.

This book is replete with examples of how designers and builders have done things you don't want in your house—they just plain make living there less enjoyable. These examples are all things that were seen in new houses, mostly spec houses and tract models, but in some custom houses, too. Custom builders are generally the same ones who build spec houses and tracts so, unless you intervene, you'll get these same flaws in your house.

The Riskiest Part

The most difficult part of the whole process, and the riskiest, is in finding a builder who is honest and open, and competent. If the builder's only interest is to see how much money he can make on the deal, it'll end up being costly for you almost regardless of what you do. On the other hand, if you get an honest builder with integrity and competency, it will still be a lot of work but the result will be a user-friendly house at the price you intended to pay. Chapter 12 discusses the means to use to find a builder.

Which gets us to an admonition that you've heard before, *Caveat Emptor* or Buyer Beware. This could never be applied more directly and unreservedly than to buying a home. There are just too many people involved, all of whom are trying to make a living, for you to assume that they are there primarily for your benefit. Most are honest enough, but their objectives and yours are not, by the nature of things, the same. So never forget, *Caveat Emptor*.

Buyers, builders, and designers don't necessarily have the same perspectives about a house.

User-Friendly Houses

A dictionary definition of value is "the desirability or worth of a thing; intrinsic worth; utility." User-friendly houses have value. The utility or usefulness of a house is directly related to how well its design and construction reflect the needs of the users.

What you'll note in the following chapters is that some of the items we discuss would cost the builder absolutely nothing to do the user-friendly way. Many more are low-cost items you'd be happy to pay for if you were given the opportunity. Being sure your house is user-friendly is a problem for the buyer simply because many designers and builders don't think that way. They're in business to sell plans and houses and they are not held responsible for the user-friendliness of what they sell. That's up to you.

Resale

When we buy, we may have no intention to move again. Yet realistically we know that's not likely to be the case. We live in a mobile society; most of us move after living in a house for less than 10 years. (Why do you think there are so many real estate agents?) Eventual resale is something you should keep in mind right from the start.

If you invest in a car, you're concerned about its resale value. If you invest in the stock market, the resale value of the stock is of the utmost importance. Yet when you consider an investment that will take a big hunk of your income for as long as you own the house, how much time do you spend in considering its resale value? The importance of this will come home to roost when you decide it is time to move and suddenly find that, while your house is your dream, it's not anyone else's. Give a little thought to this before you build; it can ease a lot of pain later. The book includes reminders about the investment side of your new home.

Regional Differences

Closely tied to the resale value of your house are the anomalies of regional differences. These are things that are done one way in one place and differently in another. In at least some builders' minds these regional preferences are so important that they simply will not go against them. In some cases these differences came about due to climatic variations between regions. In others, and this is the usual case, the differences exist simply because that's how it's been done for years and years.

A state building code official had another word for it: traditionalism. Call it what you want, these differences are not always to your advantage. In Arizona, for example, the shelf in an under-the-counter cabinet typically starts 6 to 8 inches back from the front of the cabinet, significantly reducing the amount of storage available in the cabinet. In California, you'll have to special order pull-out shelves in your cabinets, because they're not included as a rule, even in upscale houses. And in some areas, don't look for medicine cabinets in bathrooms—they're just not there.

For cases like these, you can choose to not follow the local custom and never be sorry. For some of the others, however, it may be to your disadvantage to buck the local way of doing things. You have to be careful to distinguish between doing something that's simply unusual and that which clashes with the locally established traditions. When you get too far off the beaten path, it may mean a tough resale when the time comes. (On the other hand, a house without the user-unfriendly local customs may be a welcome change for many buyers.)

Building Codes

If you're moving from one state to another or in some cases from one part of the same state to another, there's a further Buyer Beware impact. For example, California, Oregon, and Washington have state-wide building codes that, while different, all use model codes as their bases and to a large extent are the same or similar. Arizona, Idaho, and Nevada, however, don't have statewide codes and leave it up to the local governmental jurisdictions. This, in turn, can mean that there may not be any building codes in some areas. Wherever you're moving be doubly careful that you know what the local officials are enforcing, if anything.

There's a misconception that building codes will protect you from the builder's misdeeds. A central California building official told me that he receives many calls from irate homeowners about something builders have done. The building officials and inspectors have a difficult time convincing the homeowners that there's nothing government can do about it.

Building codes are directed toward health, safety, and energy conservation. They also include requirements meant to protect you from defects you can't see but which could cause safety or health problems over time. They're not intended to protect you from a builder's ineptness, dishonesty, or lack of concern about how you will enjoy life in your new house. Appendix B explains more about building and energy codes.

Getting Professional Advice

You may want advice about what kind of house you want to build or whether to buy a particular lot, but you don't want to commit to a particular builder early in the process. Some unscrupulous buyers will approach a builder with such questions, pretending they plan to work with the builder all the way to completion of the house. The builder then spends many hours of his time working up prices and going back to the buyer with the answers only to find out that the buyer wasn't serious or had planned on going out to competitive bid all along. Many builders, to protect themselves, will require some kind of deposit before they lift a finger. The deposit is forfeited if the buyer doesn't continue with the builder, otherwise it's applied to the price of the house. In effect, if you don't continue with the builder, you're paying him a consulting fee for his efforts. It's a fair arrangement.

Being Your Own Contractor

If you want to go one step further and skip the builder altogether, this can be done, even by people who have never been in the building business. There are companies whose business it is to make this possible. They help you through the process of financing, getting a house design, finding a lot, getting permits, keeping track of money, selecting subcontractors and getting them under contract. They have experienced staff who visit the job site at appropriate times to check that the subcontractors are doing what they're supposed to do. They are referred to here as "we-help-you" companies.

The help you get differs from one company to another. Don't forget *Caveat Emptor* and, before you make a commitment, check them out carefully in terms of fees, services, and the amount of money you should expect to save by doing most of the administrative functions yourself. Most importantly, check out how happy their previous clients are with the company and the house.

It's a way of parlaying your own business management capabilities into getting your custom house built less expensively. It takes a significantly higher level of involvement on your part but it's also a way to have more money in the bank when the job is done.

Problems

A responsibility you assume when you are your own general contractor is handling problems caused by subcontractors' misdeeds.

Let's take an example. You specify that you want a light switch placed in a certain place. When the electrician does his work, he ignores the specification and puts the switch where it's most convenient for him. You aren't watching things as closely as you might and the wallboard is up, textured, and painted before you see the gaff. It turns out that you wanted that wall for a special thing-a-ma-jig you brought back from Afghanistan and the switch is now right in the way. Moving the switch is the electrician's responsibility. But who pays for ripping out the wallboard, and after the switch is moved, replacing the wallboard, texturing it, and repainting the wall? Depending upon the details of your contract with the electrician, he may pay for it, otherwise you do. If you have a builder, however, that problem is the builder's, not yours. Be sure you understand your responsibilities before you decide to do it yourself.

Making it User Friendly

You won't be able to depend on the we-help-you company to make your house user-friendly. You have to do that yourself, starting with the architect/designer and following through to the last dollop of paint. This was brought forcibly to my attention when visiting an open house. The house design was by a well-known local firm that had been suggested by the we-help-you company. The master bedroom was a disaster area. Double doors opened over light switches. The door going into the bathroom opened across another door and the closet door swung into the bedroom when it could just as easily have swung into the closet without interfering with anything. (These kinds of problems are discussed in more detail in Chapter 6.) This house was not user-friendly. So, while being your own general contractor can be satisfying and economical, you must never forget: *Caveat Emptor.*

"A doctor can bury his mistakes, but an architect can only advise his clients to plant vines."

Frank Lloyd Wright

Chapter 2

Selecting a Lot

Two criteria for selecting a lot are location and price. Location involves such things as length of commute to work, suitability of schools, neighborhood, distance to shopping, and taxes. Some lots are special because of the view they offer. Other locations may be important for personal reasons.

CC&Rs

CC&Rs (Covenants, Conditions, and Restrictions) can be crucial when you consider a lot. (These are discussed in detail in Appendix A.) They restrict what you can do on a lot, even what kind of house you can build on it. You'll have to sign a document acknowledging that you've received a copy of the CC&Rs before you get title to your lot. DON'T WAIT UNTIL THEN TO READ THEM. As a rule, sales agents don't mention CC&Rs; you'll probably have to ask. Before you buy your property, read Appendix A and then read the CC&Rs. There might be some constraints, or lack of them, that would make the property unacceptable to you.

Special Assessments

As a result of the loss of revenue from Proposition 13, cities in California were hampered in their ability to build streets and put in sewers and other utilities for new subdivisions. To get around this, the state passed legislation to allow cities to set up special assessment districts so that the house buyers in new subdivisions would pay for their own streets, sewers, etc. This is commonly called "Mello-Roos" after the two legislators who sponsored the bill. If you're buying in California be sure to check for special assessments associated with the lot. It can come as a shock when you get the first tax bill and find a large, totally unexpected, special assessment payment. Not all sales agents are quick to volunteer the information—it could make you decide to look elsewhere. Ask!

The House and the Lot

When considering a lot, try to visualize how the house will fit on it. Will there be enough room on the sides or from front to back? Usually there are local constraints, either CC&Rs or building codes, on the amount of front and back setbacks required. Suppose you want room for a garden or an RV pad between your house and the adjoining one. Will your house fit on the lot?

If there are or will be houses on adjacent lots, check how much privacy you'll have. Wooden fences, common in the western states, might be all you'll need. When the adjacent house is two story or when it's above yours on a hillside, you might not want other people to have a full view of your back or side yard.

Check the orientation of the house relative to the sun and the street. The street usually dictates how the house will sit on the lot. If you've already decided on a floor plan, visualize where the afternoon sun will hit the house. Sometimes reversing the plan will make the arrangement acceptable; other times you may decide that the lot and the house just aren't compatible.

Some state energy codes allow less insulation in a house that has a high proportion of glass on the south facing side. This can lower the cost of your house. A builder or building designer should be able to advise you.

Hillside Lots

Hillside lots are attractive because they usually include a view. You can expect to pay a premium for these lots in two ways: 1) the price will be higher than other comparably sized lots, and 2) you'll have to move more dirt and pour more concrete than is normally required. If the lot is remote, there are other considerations which we'll discuss in a later section. A builder can give you some idea about the extra cost.

When you build on a hillside lot and the garage is cut back into the hillside, you may be giving up a side garage door. You should factor this into your planning.

Ground Water

How can you tell if ground water is present? If the lot hasn't been graded clear of vegetation, be suspicious when you see a heavy thicket of greenery. Ask to see any engineering reports made on the lot or the subdivision. Talk to neighboring property owners to see if they've had water problems during the rainy season.

The presence of ground water will usually mean extra expenses for foundation and drainage.

Soil

Some soils cost extra to prepare. Rock is costly to move and sandy soils may require larger footings. You can't put a foundation on uncompacted fill (dirt dumped on the lot and not packed down). You'll have to remove the fill so you can place the foundation on solid ground. All of this costs money you should know about before you buy the lot. The safest thing is to have soil samples taken, but this, too, costs money. However, it's a way of getting assurance that there won't be surprises when the bulldozer arrives. To be on the safe side, make any offer on the lot contingent on your approval of the soil study results. Or, agree to pay for the soil study only if the results are okay.

Grading and Drainage

You'll need adequate drainage from the lot. If the lot is below street level one of two things are needed:

- A sump pump to get the water back up to the storm drain in the street. Sump pumps are noisy and cause maintenance headaches when they're in the crawl space.

- An easement so that a drain line can be run across an adjacent downhill lot to a street below. Check to see if the easement exists.

Also, check what happens to water from an adjacent lot located above yours. If it runs on to your lot, ask what's being done about it. If you're not entirely satisfied, find another lot—or you may be faced with a lake in your yard when the rains come.

Another concern you should have with the grading of your lot is the steepness of the driveway into the garage. Steep driveways have two problems: 1) if there's an abrupt change in slope, part of your car will drag, usually a bumper or exhaust pipe, and 2) in icy or snowy weather you may not be able to use your garage.

Utility Boxes

Utility boxes are often forgotten when people look at a piece of property. In new developments with utility wiring run underground, the power company must put their transformers someplace. In some areas these may be underground but, if they're not, they're an eyesore, particularly if the box housing the transformer is in front of your house. Similarly, above-ground boxes for TV distribution amplifiers and telephone junction boxes, while not as big as power transformers, will look better on the front of someone else's lot.

These are among the utility boxes that look better in front of someone else's home.

You don't have much to say about where utility boxes will be located, but at least you can see where they are when it comes time to select a lot. Likewise, groupings of mail boxes furnished by the Postal Service aren't things of beauty, and would be better placed away from your lot. Don't forget that when it comes time to sell, prospective buyers will see things like this.

Far-sighted land developers can do something to reduce the visual impact of these utilitarian things. In tracts in Tacoma, Washington and Oxnard, California, subdividers built housings around utilitarian-looking mail boxes. These cosmetic housings significantly improve the appearance of the boxes.

Traffic Noise

Traffic and traffic noise will impact the selling value of the property.

- We moved into our house in northern California when the nearby freeways had little traffic. When we put the house on the market 15 years later, we had more than one prospective buyer pull up in front of the house, stop, listen, and get back into the car and drive off.

- A couple we know chose a lot in a large subdivision when the builder was just starting construction. It was close to the golf course clubhouse, making it convenient for golf, dinner at the club, and the other social amenities they desired. The lot backed up onto a street that had no traffic; in fact, it dead-ended just a block away. A quiet, ideal place to spend their retirement years.

Slowly over the next several years they found out what the sales agent hadn't told them. Their quiet dead-end street was no longer quiet or dead-end. As the subdivision grew, so had the street, both in length and in volume of traffic. It became, in fact, a very busy arterial. They have decided to put up with the noise rather than go through the stress of moving again. But the reminder is always there—you can't be too careful when choosing the location for your home

Take the time to find out what future traffic patterns are planned around any lot you consider. Stay as far away from freeways as you can and at least a block away from what could become a major arterial.

Corner Lots

If you buy a corner lot, be sure the garage side of the house is away from the corner. You may have to reverse the floor plan to do this. There are several reasons:

- It's safer to back the car out of the driveway.

- The side of the house away from the garage is often more attractive as seen from the street.

- The garage side is where you're more likely to have an RV pad and garbage cans—items you'd rather not have on the street side of the house.

Zero Lot Lines

Some subdivisions use zero lot lines, meaning one wall of each house is located on a property line. In some cases, two houses share a common wall, so that from the street the two houses look like a duplex. In other cases, each house is separate, with all houses in the block placed on the same side of their lots.

It's unlikely you'll find such a lot for sale; usually the subdivider is the only one who builds on them. If you do run across a lot like this, be careful to understand all that it entails. There will be some definite restrictions on where and what you can build.

A word of caution about zero-lot-line tracts. They are, of necessity, associated with a homeowners' association, which is responsible for street-side landscape maintenance and fire insurance. The homeowners' association dues can be sizable.

Country Lots

When the lot you're considering is outside a metropolitan area, you need to remember water, sewers, gas, electricity, telephone, and roads. If you need to drill a well, you need a back-up plan in case the water you get is not potable. If you require a septic tank and leach field, you need to know that the soil is suitable. The seller may be able to guarantee these things; otherwise make any offer on the lot subject to your approval of test results.

Before making an offer on such a lot, find out what the utility companies will charge to get power, gas, and telephone to the lot. Also, find out what the costs will be to have a road extended to it.

Owners of houses in the country, or even in the city adjacent to an undeveloped area, need to be concerned about the danger of wild fires. What happened in Oakland in 1991 gave many Californians food for thought. The result is that a number of jurisdictions in the state enacted additional local building codes. These require that homes built where there is a danger of wild fires take extra precautions to prevent the house from burning. Be sure to check what this may mean in extra building costs. It can, for example, be prohibitively expensive to run the water line for a fire hydrant to your lot.

Easements

Find out if there are any easements on the lot and, if so, what they mean to you. Sometimes the easement means you have to give up any use of part of your property; other times it means you can't use it for some purposes. Find out before you buy.

- Don't be like one couple who was shown a lot by a real estate salesperson. It and the neighborhood suited them fine. On the plot plan in the office they noted an easement across the back of the lot but thought little of it. When it came time to build, they discovered the easement was a ditch 6 feet wide and 3 feet deep. They can't just fill it in because it's for rain water that flows all winter. They're now looking at an expensive drain line and having fill dirt hauled in if they want to use the rest of their lot.

"Form ever follows function."

Louis H. Sullivan

Chapter 3

Designers and House Designs

When you start to plan for your new house, some terms can be confusing. We'll start this chapter by running over some of them.

Floor plans are scale diagrams of the layout of the rooms, halls, etc. in a house. There will be separate drawings for each floor. House design packages include floor plans along with other drawings from which a builder can build the house.

Building Designers

People who make house designs may be architects, who are registered in the state where they work, or designers who generally aren't required to be registered. Architects are usually graduates of a school of architecture who must pass a series of tests given by the state. Most belong to a national professional organization, the American Institute of Architects (AIA).

The American Institute of Building Designers (AIBD) is an organization of designers. Some states, including Arizona, California, Oregon, and Washington, have state societies. The AIBD conducts a certification program for designers who must meet requirements of experience and pass a two-day written examination. Note that, while it isn't necessary for a designer to be certified or even to belong to the AIBD in order to be in the business of making house designs, certification suggests that the individual may have qualifications not possessed by other designers.

In our discussions here, anyone who designs houses is called a designer without distinction among registered architects, AIBD members, certified or not, and others.

We distinguish between the designer who has existing plans for sale, usually found in catalogs, magazines, and newspapers, and the designer who makes a custom design just for you.

Designers Who Sell Existing Plans

Some newspapers publish a floor plan in the Sunday issue to interest readers and advertise for the designer. In front of me is one such floor plan. The master bedroom doesn't have enough wall space for furniture, the walk-in closet door is in the way when open, doors block other doors, and the galley-style kitchen has little counter space. The artist's drawing of the exterior doesn't match the floor plan. Dimensions given for rooms don't match the plan. In effect, this whole Home of the Week is an insult to the intelligence of the reader.

Very few floor plans are this bad. This example is used to emphasize that the only purpose for the floor plans seen in newspapers, magazines, and catalogs is to sell house designs. Unfortunately, it's often the glitz that sells plans, not what's behind it. Designers eat when plans sell and they go hungry when they don't.

In the long run, many design firms become successful when they develop good reputations. However, there are some that stay in business because of their marketing techniques rather than from providing good designs. Learn to be skeptical so you can cut through the verbiage that surrounds the house plans you see advertised. Treat it like all other advertising—look past the words to the product itself. This is tough to do if you think of the designers as the experts and of yourself as an ignoramus in the matter of floor plans.

The Custom Designer

The biggest problem you will have, if you decide to use a custom designer, is to find the right one for you. As in all professions, there are good and bad practitioners. Not all good designers are architects (nor are all architects good designers). Designers may be graduates of the same school of architecture as the architects.

So how do you find the architect or designer for you? Like finding a good builder, it's a tough proposition. The first step should be to decide what you want. Look at as many custom houses as you can and, when you see something you like, find out who designed it. Ask people in the building business for recommendations, particularly builders who only build custom houses (as distinguished from those who build spec houses until they can get a custom job). When you talk to a designer, find out what their strong points are. If these are in line with what you have in mind, ask for a list of houses they've designed. If possible, ask the designer to arrange for you to talk to the people now living in them. Find out how much the designer works with their clients and how many decisions they make on their own without the client's input. The house should be what you want, not what the designer thinks is good for you.

Listen to the designer—they have much more experience than you. A good designer not only draws up plans and specifications, he or she is your consultant in the whole process. If you choose, you can have them be your eyes on site during the construction process. But you probably won't want to spend the money to have them there as often as is really necessary to ensure that things go according to your plans. You should be the one who visits the site frequently.

When working with the designer, don't forget all of the user-unfriendly things you now know to look for. Keep this book handy. It's up to you to watch for and insist on getting a user-friendly house.

The Artistic Designer

Watch out for the dramatic design. Occasionally the designer, in an effort to be *avant-garde*, will come up with designs in which pent-up artistic drive overshadows the need for practicality. The result is, too often, a work of art that is not very livable. This can happen in houses in any price range, but is more likely to occur in higher-priced ones.

• In one upscale house in Salem, Oregon, the building designer, interior designer, and builder decided to leave the microwave oven out of the kitchen design. The range, including oven and cooktop, was built into an island so that there was no appliance in the upper cabinets anyplace in the kitchen. To install a built-in microwave oven would have destroyed the 'flow' of the kitchen. So it was left out.

The home user will have to be content with a counter-top unit. And just where is the flow with a large unit like that sitting on top of the counter? In this case the designers forgot that the kitchen is a place to live in. Countertops are working areas. They get cluttered up fast enough. Large items like microwave ovens do not belong on them.

The Non-Professional Designer

Professional building designers, at least the good, responsible ones, have had many years of experience in which to learn from their mistakes. The sometime designer-builder and people who design their own houses simply don't have that experience. And it shows. True, many house plans sold by professional designers include things that shouldn't be the way they are. But the conclusion, from looking at hundreds of houses, is that the person who makes the most flagrant goofs is the one who isn't a full-time designer.

Any designer's starting place is his own knowledge. This comes from formal training and/or experience. The problem with the non-professional designer is that this knowledge is too meager. The resulting plans show personal likes and dislikes, things that are important only to him or her.

The Builder-Designer—When the self-styled designer is also a builder who doesn't know or care about high quality, you have a situation that's about as bad as it gets. Almost as bad is the builder who takes a designer's plans and changes things here and there to save money, incorporate a pet amenity, or 'improve' on the design. In a well-designed house there are reasons things are the way they are. Moving, eliminating, or adding something compromises the overall integrity of the design. More often than not, these changes cause other problems.

- The real estate agent, in one house I visited, also claimed to be a builder. She had some very definite opinions about a number of things, including refrigerators. When I commented that a side-by-side refrigerator would not do well in the particular kitchen design, she said in no uncertain terms that that didn't matter. She had a separate freezer in her garage and didn't need or want a side-by-side unit. By implication, it didn't matter whether a kitchen could accommodate a side-by-side unit.

When builders design their own floor plans, be especially careful.

- In one two-story house I saw, a designer-builder had several nice features not usually seen in houses in the price range. But the realtor who was with me and I could hardly believe our eyes. In fact, we both took a double trip around the upstairs to be sure.

The house had only one upstairs bathroom for all of the house's three bedrooms! It was large as bathrooms go, with separate doors into it from the hall and master bedroom. This is just not done in today's houses. Not surprisingly, the house was still for sale several months later.

- In another case where the builder did the design himself, the house was on the market for many months during a time when other builders were selling their houses as fast as they could put them up. This house is a tri-level arrangement with the kitchen, dining room, and living room on the middle level and the bedrooms on the upper level.

OSHA didn't see this one, but I did, in a builder-designed house.

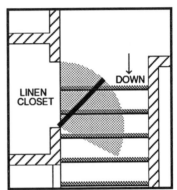

Right next to the top of the stairs going up to the bedrooms is the linen closet. This closet has a full-sized hinged door on it. It faces the stairs and, when the door is opened, it swings out over the stairs. It is just plain dangerous. If OSHA had to approve houses, this one wouldn't have made it.

- In yet another builder-designed house a large picture window comes down to the floor right beside the toilet! It is rare to have a view from a toilet. The arrangement is unusual to say the least.

A caution here is to consider eventual resale. Houses with such off-beat features aren't likely to be sold easily.

Don't Do the Design Yourself

It is suggested that you do not try to do your own house design. Books have been published that encourage readers to design houses with the help given in the books. People often try this. It is usually not a good idea. As noted above, the worst floor plans, the ones with the most defects, are those done by people with the least experience. This is not surprising. There are many, many factors to be taken into account to get a floor plan that is user-friendly, attractive, code-compliant, and cost-effective. The items discussed in this book will be a help in this respect. But the book is not a "How-to" manual for designing a house. If you're brave, you can try to get that from other books. Or, better, draw on the expertise of a competent, professional building designer.

Interior Designers

Among the other decisions that have to be made are those that take a building design and turn it into a livable house. These include colors, wall coverings, floor coverings, cabinets, countertops, lighting fixtures, and many more. These aspects make up the interior design and the artist who puts it all together is the interior designer.

As with building designers, interior designers have their own professional associations. The two you are most likely to come across are the American Society of Interior Designers and the International Society of Interior Designers. These groups have certification programs for members that give some assurance of professional experience and competency. At present there is no provision for state registration of interior designers.

What Interior Designers Do

The interior designer takes the shell of the building as it comes from the building designer and makes it into a livable house. Or at least that's the way it can work. Some folks who call themselves designers simply don't have the competency to do this. At other times they're called into the house design process after a number of the interior design decisions have already been made by either the buyer or the building designer.

Oftentimes the builder, working with the buyer, will make the interior design decisions without the services of an interior designer. Designers, however, can be of a great deal of assistance to you. They should know what materials are available and how to pick them so that the interior of the house is seen as an entity and not as a bunch of rooms under a single roof. They can make decisions that avoid many of the user-unfriendly things discussed in this book. If you're short of time or feel uncomfortable trying to remember all the things that need to be considered, and you have the money for the services of a competent interior designer, consider it a good investment.

An interior designer works much more closely with the home buyer in considering the aesthetics of the home than does the building designer who is more of a nuts and bolts person.

The skills of good interior designers are many and varied. They must be able to ferret out your likes and dislikes. They must know what materials are available, what's good, what's bad and what it costs. They must have a sense of totality, of what works together to create a whole. And they must know what makes a house user friendly and their designs must reflect this knowledge.

Selecting an Interior Designer

There are two criteria for selecting an interior designer: do they do good work and are you comfortable with them? Talk to people who have used an interior designer. Look at work the designer has done and see if it looks coordinated and consistent. You won't want to use the same things in your house but, if previous design work jars you or if it seems too boring or a mishmash, it's a warning that the designer may not be good at doing things you like.

Ideally, the building designer and the interior designer should work together from the start. Often what the interior designer would like to do is compromised by something in the house design that could be easily changed on paper but not later. A window size or shape, for example, is usually arbitrary on the part of the building designer but can make all the difference in the world in what the interior designer can do. If you are going to include an interior designer in your design team, get him or her in on the project early.

House Plans

A set of house plans includes a floor plan and as much other design information as the designer feels is necessary for a reasonably competent builder to get the house built. The detail varies considerably from one design company to another. House plans include floor plans, elevations (how the house looks from each side), a foundation plan, a framing plan, details of the roof framing, an electrical plan, and drawings showing the details of any special construction techniques that are needed. If you have a designer work with you to put together a set of plans for your house on your lot, there will also be a site plan showing where the house goes and some of the exterior considerations such as driveways, RV pads, sidewalks, patios, and decks.

If the house is structurally unusual, the designer may be required to use the services of a structural engineer to satisfy the requirements of the local building officials. For some houses, you or the designer may decide to bring an interior designer into the design team. Interior designers are discussed later in this chapter.

Be aware of the tendency of some builders and their subcontractors to wing it. Some of these not-according-to-plan activities can result in things that are not user-friendly (as, for example, electricians who have their own ideas of where switches should go). Whether you use an existing set of drawings or use a set drawn up especially for you, the more detail you have in the drawings and in the accompanying specifications, the better chance you have of getting things your way. (This is not to say that if the electrician or the plumber has some ideas of his own you shouldn't listen to them. Take good advice any place you can get it.) But, insofar as possible, plan on figuring out just what you want and spelling it out in gruesome detail, whether you are working with a single builder or writing a set of specifications to get bids from several.

- During construction of a house that she designed, an architect caught the heating subcontractor just in time. She'd made a special effort to put the return air grill in an inconspicuous place and this was spelled out in the house design package. The subcontractor's people hadn't bothered to read it, they were going ahead just like they always had. Of course, they could have been made to change it later but this could have been a real mess if the wallboard had already been put in place and the texturing done.

- In the same house, the architect had left a wall space where a painting could be hung. She indicated the general area where an electrical switch should go. The electrician put the switch, not near the corner of the wall where it would normally be expected, but well into the area where the picture had been planned. This one wasn't caught in time.

The moral of these two examples is that you can't be too vigilant. Write specifications down in fine detail and then watch that the builder and the subcontractors do what they're supposed to do. It has been said that when some builders and/or their subs find out that an architect is involved, they'll automatically increase the size of their bids simply because they now have to pay attention to what they are doing. If you want things done your way, you should specify what you want in writing, and then insist that the specifications be followed.

Assessing Existing House Designs

Be particularly careful about buying plans from a different part of the country. Full basements on flat lots, for example, are common in much of the country and virtually unseen in the west. The type of construction will be different among houses designed to have a basement, a crawl space, or a slab floor. Another thing to be careful about is that some houses are designed to use 4-inch exterior walls and others to use 6-inch. If the house is to be in an area that has energy codes, it will probably require 6-inch walls.

Sometimes plans can be modified for use in your area but it is much more straightforward to find one that is designed for your part of the country. There are literally thousands of house designs available for sale. It's likely that, with a little patience and perseverance, you can find one you like, that fits your budget, and that requires little or no modifications.

At one time it was a common practice to include the closet, vanity, shower, tub, and toilet areas in the dimensions for the master bedroom. Some of these old plans are still being sold. Be careful and, if you can, use an architect's scale to check dimensions if the numbers in the floor plan don't seem right.

Keep these three things in mind when you're looking at existing plans:

1. The designer isn't going to be living in the house, you are.

2. It's your money that's being invested in the house, not his.

3. He's trying to sell plans, you're trying to fulfill a dream.

Floor Plans

The remainder of this book includes many of the things you should have in mind when you look at floor plans. A few others are considered here. But remember that the only place to catch design flaws is at the floor-plan stage—once construction starts it's usually too late.

One Story or Two?

In deciding between a one- and a two-story plan, consider:

• Stairs.
• Space taken by stairs.

- Heating and cooling.
- Lot requirements.
- Shading from roof overhangs.

Stairs—Older people, even those without physical disabilities, prefer not having stairs to go up and down. Two-story plans with the master bedroom on the first floor are helpful but most often single-floor plans are the choice of senior citizen.

Space Taken by Stairs—A typical stairwell, including framing, is 4' × 13' which is over 100 square feet (50 on each floor) of useless space. Landings also take away from the useful floor area.

Overall, the single floor house will often be lower priced for the same amount of useful square footage. Don't assume that a two-story house is a better buy until you take out the floor space lost to stairs and landings.

Heating and Cooling—Be aware that the upstairs rooms are noticeably warmer than downstairs areas. Most builders don't do anything about this even through there are ways to correct it. It will cost money and this should be taken into account when comparing one- and two-story houses.

Lot Requirements—For the same amount of useful floor area, the two-story house can take up less of the lot. If this is important, it may be the deciding criterion in selecting your floor plan.

Shading—Roof overhangs can be used to shade windows on one-story buildings but not the lower windows of two-story houses. This could be particularly important in the desert and other hot climates.

How Many Square Feet?

The best practice when comparing houses is to look at the actual room sizes and see which best fits your needs. The number of square feet on a floor plan is only a general guide. In many plans there is useless space that still costs to build and heat. The following discussion addresses some of these areas. How they affect your ideas about a particular house design is a personal matter.

The square footage of a house is measured from the outside of the house and includes all the area taken up by outside walls themselves. It's generally believed that two-story houses are less expensive per square foot than are one story buildings because of the smaller foundations and roofs. This is true if you stop right there.

The effect of stairs was noted earlier, but they aren't the only place where unused space is included in the overall square footage. Some master bedrooms have many square feet in the center of the room which serve no useful purpose other than to make the room look bigger. Even kitchens sometimes end up with space that isn't used. This is unfortunate, because it will take many more steps to work in such a kitchen than would have been needed if the design had been done right.

- In one house in Salem, Oregon, the space allocated for the breakfast eating area was small and the builder decided to add a larger breakfast nook by a window on the other side of the kitchen. But the original space was left unused, a large open area with no obviously useful purpose unless it's to provide exercise in walking through it.

Other places to look for useless space are in the centers of walk-in closets and pantries. To be sure, you need to have a place to stand, but good design will minimize the amount of space required. Eliminating the walk-in pantry is one way to avoid the waste. Cabinet-type pantries with pull-out shelves make much better use of the space than does a walk-in unit.

You'll often find unused space in hallways. Some plans tie up a lot more space in hallways than do others. A second-story bridge that goes across an open space between two upstairs bedrooms is an example of totally unused space.

Design Considerations

Simplicity

In general, the simpler the outside of the house, the less expensive it will be. A simple rectangular box will be more economical to build than a house with notches and zigzags in the walls. Similarly, the more complex the roof line, the more costly it will be to erect. Steeply pitched roofs can be more expensive than those of moderate pitch because of the greater difficulty (and danger) for the roofer to work on a steep roof.

Siting

Be sure your floor plan will fit the lot. Look at the proposed front, back, and side yards. Consider the driveway and the front walk. Look at the house relative to the sun. It's an axiom in the designer's world that the kitchen should face east. North facing kitchens lack sunshine all of the time, while south and west facing kitchens get the summer sun when you don't want it.

General Considerations

The floor plan should make the house feel comfortable and easy to live in. Look at which areas will get the most use and where people will walk when getting from one area to another. Is the traffic path through the kitchen where culinary efforts are under way? Is there a lot of traffic across the family room in front of the TV? It takes only a few minutes to decide if a floor plan makes sense in terms of how the house will be used.

Consider the room arrangement and noise. Family rooms next to bedrooms can be a problem unless the wall between is sound insulated.

Is there an entry closet? Surprisingly, some designs don't include them. The same thing goes for linen closets. These are often in hallways or, sometimes, in bathrooms. And, sometimes, there aren't any at all!

Is the garage close to the kitchen? When it is, it makes for shorter trips from the car to the living area of the house, particularly with groceries and trash. In some house designs the garage can do a good job of shielding part of the house from midday or afternoon sun or winter storms if it's on the right side of the house.

If you're planning a two-story house, be sure to include a half-bath downstairs.

Bedrooms over the garage are virtually impossible to insulate against the noise of the opening and closing of the garage doors. Think twice before using plans that have this arrangement.

Is there a door out the back of the house? Surprisingly, some plans forget this. In other cases, the way out to the back is through the garage but the garage lacks a side door!

These are a few of the things which you should think about in selecting the design of your new home. The next several chapters discuss many more considerations that impact on the house design.

Part II

The Whole-House Systems

Electrical
Heating
Plumbing
Doors
Interiors
Windows
Closets
Floors
Storage

Chapter 4

The Electrical System

In this and following chapters, the discussions are about systems which are whole-house in nature, i.e., that involve the entire house rather than a single room or area. As with every part of the house, decisions must be made about what's in these systems and where they are to go. If you make the decisions, you control what you get; if you leave it to the builder and his subs, you'll get what they want.

Electrical Specifications

As in other things, the more precise you are in what you want, the better. In your specifications, include specific brands and model numbers of all major appliances and materials, otherwise the builder can be expected to provide the lowest priced items available, which may not be what you want. Don't hesitate to go against the "in" thing of the moment if it is not to your liking or if it is something you believe is a momentary fad.

Because you see the same thing in house after house doesn't mean it's user-friendly. Microwave ovens mounted over single-unit stoves are good examples. These ovens include an exhaust system, making them less costly to buy and install and doing away with the often unattractive hood over the cooktop. Unfortunately the exhaust system in these ovens is not particularly effective. Popularity doesn't necessarily equate to usefulness.

Oftentimes decisions on some of the items discussed below are left to the electrician. Don't hesitate to make your wants known in writing, in detail. This may annoy the electrician, but so what? He's not going to be living in the house, you are.

Switches and Outlets

Which type of wall switches will you want, the older flip switches or the more modern rocker switches? They both work fine but the rocker switches are perceived by many as being easier to use and being more in keeping with today's home designs. The rocker switches are a little more expensive but are still a small cost item in the overall cost of a home.

What color do you want the switches, outlets, TV connector plates, and telephone jack plates? There should be no difference in cost. These are among the few things which can be changed after you've moved in without tearing the house apart. But it'll cost less if it's done right the first time.

Switch Location

Be very specific about switch locations. Electricians sometimes have their own ideas. In one house, for instance, the horizontal distance from the room entry to the light switch varies throughout the house, more or less randomly, between 3¼" and 17½". It's a real pain trying to find a light switch in the dark.

When there are gaps of an inch to a foot between two or more switches on a wall, someone was careless. Specify what you want and insist that the switches be grouped in the same electrical box, not scattered here and there. (This includes gas fireplace controls; they can and should be put with the other switches and controls that are on the same wall.)

Mark on the electrical plan exactly where you want the switches and wall-mounted controls for the various lights, fans, and gas fireplaces. As a rule, insist that the switches be mounted in the room with the light, outlet, or appliance they control and that they be within 6" of the entry to the room or hall. (This may mean that the framers have to pay more attention than usual to where they put studs. So be it, it's your house.)

In the case of gas fireplaces, the on-off switch should be close to the fireplace. If there is a separate switch or speed control for the fireplace fan, it should be in the same mounting box as the on-off switch. If there is another switch in the vicinity, use the same box for all the switches. Alternatively, you can have them separated as is commonly done is some parts of the Pacific Northwest.

One electrician's idea of how to put three switches on a wall.

Specify how high off the floor you want the switches and outlets. 45" is normal for switches and controls and 12" for outlets.

Don't forget switches for lights in closets and pantries. These items are easily overlooked until the house is built—when it's too late to fix.

• In one house, the switch is on the wall on the outside of the walk-in pantry but it's on the hinged side of the door. To use the pantry, it is necessary to walk completely around the door after turning on the light.

• In another example, the light switch is inside the pantry where it belongs—except a shelf was installed just above the switch so that you have to lean over to reach it. Be alert to keep such annoying and unfriendly workmanship out of your house.

Switches and Stairs

Lights for stairs normally use a 3-way switch with one switch at the top and one at the bottom of the stairs. If the stair light is also used for illumination of an area at the top of the stairs (a landing, hall, or bridge) it's convenient to have an additional switch so you don't have to walk around in the dark after coming up the stairs. An arrangement where three switches are grouped so that any one of them can turn the lights on/off is called a 4-way switch.

Switches and Doors

Be careful not to place switches behind doors since people tend to leave doors open most of the time. Also watch out for pocket doors. Switches cannot be put in the pockets and, as with double doors, this can lead to putting switches in inconvenient locations.

When the builder isn't keeping on top of things, or just doesn't care, you'll find switches right behind the stair railing. This is definitely an unacceptable bit of workmanship.

A light switch behind the hand rail. This happened when an unthinking electrician and an uncaring builder got together.

Switches and Double Doors

The location of light switches is a vexing problem with double doors because you often have to take several steps after entering a room to get to the light switch. You may get used to it, but you'll never be happy about having the switch in an inconvenient location. Ideally, there should be a wall that can be reached by opening the door only 90 degrees with the light switch right at the end of the door.

- In an upper-middle-range home near Portland both doors from the hall swing a full 180 degrees into the bedroom. The light switch is behind one of the doors. There is another set of double doors between the bedroom and the bath/vanity area. Again, the light switch is behind one of the doors. There are simply better designs.

- In an expensive home in the yearly "Street of Dreams" in Portland, Oregon, the double doors into the master bedroom suite were removed for the show. It then wasn't evident that the light switch for the master bedroom and the key pad for the alarm system would be blocked by one of the doors. Here, as elsewhere, it is always better to think ahead and not put switches in inconvenient locations.

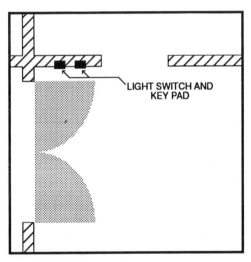

LIGHT SWITCH AND KEY PAD

Don't put switches behind doors as was done in this upscale master bedroom suite.

There were similar models in two different parts of California with double doors opening into the master bedroom. One door opens against a wall which makes an ideal location for the light switch. Instead, the switches are located where a person has to walk completely around the other door to get to the switches. Not ergonomic and not user-friendly.

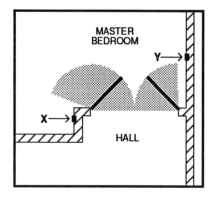

Switch should be at Y, not at X where you have to walk around the door to use it.

If you have double doors that swing 180 degrees into a bedroom or den, consider installing a 3-way arrangement using two switches. One switch goes in the hall and the other goes inside the room in a convenient place. Then the light can be turned on or off from the hall as well as inside the room. Be sure to pick the right spots for these switches. The switch in the hall should be next to the door that is normally used; the best place for the one inside will depend on the room layout.

Ceiling Fans

Appendix L, a discussion of ceiling fans, develops these recommendations:

- Insist on having a 3-conductor power cable from the fan to the switch. This is needed for separate control of the fan and a light, whether the light is included initially or is added later.

- For any ceiling fixtures that might be changed later to a ceiling fan, insist that the mounting box be made strong enough for a fan.

In Vancouver, Washington and Portland and Salem, Oregon, electricians do something unique to the region. When installing a ceiling fan with a light kit, they mount the wall controls a foot apart vertically, the light switch being at the normal height and the fan switch a foot above. (Some electricians have extended this approach to the on-off switch and fan switch for gas fireplaces.) It's a regional quirk. You can have it done in your house but it'll look strange to anyone from outside the area.

Ground-Fault Circuit-Interrupter Protection

You've probably noticed some outlets with two buttons labeled "Test" and "Reset." These are ground-fault circuit-interrupter (GFCI) protection devices designed to protect you against electrocution. See Appendix D about the impact these have on wiring in your baths, kitchen, garage, and outside the house.

Telephone and Television Wiring

The options for wiring telephones and video services are discussed in Appendix F. You need to decide:

• Locations of telephone jacks and television outlet connectors. An extra copy of the floor plan can be marked up to show where these go.

• Whether to have the telephone system wired as in the past or in a more flexible way to accommodate your needs.

• Where to have the interconnection point between the video cables from each TV outlet and the incoming cable or roof-mounted antenna.

The location for the TV outlet in the family room should be related to the location of the fireplace as discussed in Chapter 10.

In the master bedroom, the appropriate location for the TV outlet is one where you can watch the video while resting in bed. This suggests a location across the room from the head of the bed. Check out where you will put furniture in the room. If the best place for the TV is where you also want a piece of bedroom furniture then decide if you want the TV on top of the furniture.

Sound Systems

If you want the house wired for sound, include wiring requirements for the central unit and speakers as a part of the specification package. You will need to include enough details so that you can get a firm price. Work with a system supplier to write the specifications so your wishes are clear. You may want the price for the wiring or for the whole system as an option so you can include what you want when you see the cost.

"A house is a machine for living."

Buckminster Fuller

Chapter 5

Heating and Plumbing Systems

The heating, ventilation, and air conditioning (HVAC) system is discussed in the first part of this chapter; in the second part are some plumbing items which you may want to consider for your new house.

The usual set of house plans does not include drawings for either the plumbing or the HVAC systems. The HVAC and the plumbing are generally left strictly to subcontractors who work from the floor plans to figure out just what is needed in the house. HVAC subs, for example, calculate heat loss from each room through the floor, walls, windows, doors, and ceiling. From these calculations, they figure the most economic way to heat the house, including the size of the furnace and ducts. They decide where the registers should go. Then they put all this on a drawing, order the required materials and install the system

The plumber works similarly, figuring out pipe sizes, etc. Usually, there won't be a drawing to work from—it's all in the plumber's mind and some scribbles on a piece of paper. However, on large houses, houses with unusual requirements, or houses where the builder requires it, the plumber will generate a drawing.

If your requirements are simple and straightforward, you may feel comfortable letting the builder work with his subs in the usual fashion. If you have any doubts, insist that you and/or your building designer approve the drawings before the subs begin work. Remember that, if due to human error or misunderstandings, something isn't done right at the design stage, by the time you find it, it's probably too late.

Heating and Air Conditioning

The HVAC system in a new house today is much more than just a means of controlling the temperature. It, and the way the house is built, determine energy efficiency, comfort, and the size of your heating bills.

In building jargon the contractor responsible for the heating and air conditioning systems is called the mechanical contractor. He has the responsibility for the system design.

Consider this personal experience:

- The heating system in our house was designed by the mechanical subcontractor. When the cold season came we found the bedroom wing of the house was too warm and the living areas weren't warm enough. We permanently closed off the heating registers in all three bedrooms to balance the system. In trying to understand why this was necessary, I found that the basic design put about the same amount of hot air into both areas. However, while the two areas have about the same number of square feet, the living area of the house has a larger proportion of glass and outside wall than does the bedroom wing, so the living area has significantly more heat loss. The basic heating design was faulty. By closing all the bedroom registers, which we shouldn't have to do, the house is comfortable.

After it is completed, there is little that can be done and, in fact, a strong argument could be made that what's in the house is okay. However, if a knowledgeable person had reviewed the HVAC plans this wouldn't have happened. It may not always be possible to find someone to do this for you, but it is good insurance if you can.

Another reason for wanting to check the HVAC plans is to check the locations of registers. Your specs may spell out exactly what you want but, unless the mechanical sub is paying attention and understands them, his plans may not reflect your wishes.

Gas is available for heating in most places and electricity is available every place. The way the two sources of heat are used may be different. Gas systems use a central furnace and hot air is blown through ducts to the various rooms in the house. Sometimes there are separate zones of the house so that the bedrooms and the living areas can be kept at different temperatures. Electric heat, on the other hand, is often on a room-by-room basis with each room having its own control. The most common electrical heating system is used in conjunction with a heat pump as is discussed below.

"Air Conditioner Ready"

Some house ads will say "air conditioner ready." This can mean one of several things: the wiring and piping are in place ready for the air conditioner, the wiring is in place, or only that the furnace has space for adding the expander coils. Adding wiring, once the house is finished, is a fairly expensive proposition and may involve running the wiring in a conduit on the outside of the house. It's worthwhile, if there's a possibility of adding an air conditioner, to have the wiring for it put in place when the house is built. Depending on the house design, it may also be worthwhile to make the openings in the foundation or elsewhere for the pipes that go between the furnace location and the compressor outside of the house.

Heat Pumps

An increasingly popular option for heating and air conditioning is the heat pump. It is more efficient than having separate centralized heating and air conditioning. The heat pump does just as its name implies: it pumps heat from one place to another. For heating, it gathers heat from outside your house and pumps it inside. For cooling it takes the heat from inside the house and pumps it outside. Some fundamentals of heat pumps are discussed in Appendix N.

In practice, heat pumps are more expensive to buy and less expensive to operate than separate heating and cooling units. In climates where the outside air temperature gets too low for efficient winter pumping, two options are available: 1) use a gas or electric furnace backup, or 2) use the ground as the source of heat. The latter arrangement is more expensive initially, but avoids the need for backup heating.

People who use heat pumps report another concern—the pumps respond to temperature changes slowly. This is another way of saying that the amount of heat they can pump is limited. With modern, well-insulated houses, heat pumps keep up with day-to-day temperature changes quite nicely. If you are away from home for a while with the heat pump turned off, you can expect it will take longer to get the house back to normal temperature than it would with a separate furnace or air conditioner.

Which heating and cooling approach is best for you will depend on the climate in your area, whether cooling is important to you, and on gas and electric energy costs. Your local heating and air conditioning equipment supplier can best advise you. If the same utility company sells both gas and electricity, then they, too, are a good source of information. If gas and electricity come from different companies, you may not get an unbiased opinion from them.

Ducts

In one-story houses with crawl spaces, the heating/cooling ducts are usually run under the house and the registers are in the floor. With concrete slab floors, the ducts, and often the furnace also, are in the attic and the registers are in the ceiling or in walls close to the ceiling. With two stories, the registers may be in the floor or in the ceiling.

In kitchens and bathroom vanities in houses with floor registers, it is common practice to bring a heating duct up under a cabinet. A register is placed in a cutout in the front of the cabinet base to let the air into the room. This scheme avoids cutting a register into a floor area which is heavily traveled. The place where the register is located is known as the toe space. It works quite nicely—usually.

- In a classic example of the builder not paying attention, the cabinet installer forgot to cut the register into the base of the kitchen cabinet in a house. Then cold weather came and the home user noticed that the kitchen was the coldest room in the house and there was no way that enough heat could be forced into it to make it comfortable without overheating everything else.

  One day the home user, while visiting another house, noticed a register in the toe space under the kitchen sink. Sure enough, back home he found the cabinet area under the sink was toasty warm but the heat had no way to get out. After a discussion with the builder, the cabinet installer was called back to finish his job, the register was put into place, and the problem was solved.

Registers in Traffic Areas

Be sure to check register locations carefully on the HVAC drawing. It is unfortunate to find a floor register located just where you want to place a piece of furniture. The builder and the mechanical subcontractor will usually take the position that they can't foresee what furniture the owner will have nor where it will be placed.

Therefore, they use their rules-of-thumb about placing registers. So if you have any ideas of your own, let them be known early on.

Sometimes this do-it-like-we've-always-done-it approach results in things which should not happen. A common rule-of-thumb says to center the floor register in front of the room's window.

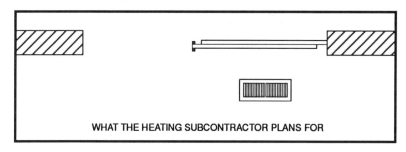

WHAT THE HEATING SUBCONTRACTOR PLANS FOR

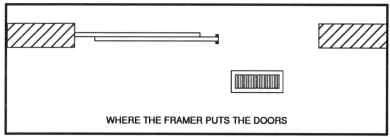

WHERE THE FRAMER PUTS THE DOORS

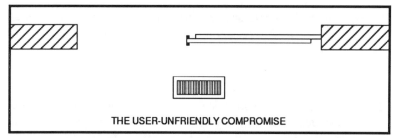

THE USER-UNFRIENDLY COMPROMISE

Heating/cooling registers in front of sliding doors are not always where they should be.

When the window is a sliding glass door, half of the register is in the entry to the room. Registers are not designed to take foot traffic nor are feet designed to walk on registers.

If you make it clear, in writing, that registers are not to be in traffic areas, it is up to the builder to see that his subs do their jobs correctly and fix it if they don't.

Builders Dirt in the Floor Registers

There is a further problem with floor registers; construction dirt and debris. The mechanical subcontractor installs the ducts at a time when much of the house is unfinished. To prevent rain and dirt from getting into the ducts, a good mechanical subcontractor seals them immediately after installation. When the outer shell of the house is completed, unless forbidden by code, the builder takes the covers off the ducts and turns the furnace on to dry out the interior. This is done before any cleanup work is done and before wallboard goes up. The result is that significant amounts of debris, dirt, and dust fall into the ducts, lying there in wait for you, the new owner, when you move in.

- The worst is the dust from wallboard work. This is very fine and can pass through the ordinary furnace filter and will be in the house forever unless you get some special filters to remove it. We were in our new house for almost two years with this fine coating of fine dust always present. Putting in a different set of furnace filters caught most of it.

When the builder is going to use the furnace for warming and drying the house during the latter phases of construction, he may do one of several things:

1. Clean out the ducts before turning the property over to the buyer.

2. Don't open the ducts until construction is complete. With this approach a portable propane heater is used to heat and dry out the house. One builder I talked to uses a dehumidifier to remove the moisture.

3. Buy a set of special air filters to go over the open registers which lets the heat through but does not let debris into the duct. These filters are removed and thrown away when the registers are put into place after construction work has been completed. They are available from Quality Air Systems, 4820 115th Avenue, Clear Lake, Minn. 55319, telephone (612) 743-2627.

4. Put caps over the ends of the ducts or the boots whenever workers are in the house and run the furnace only when they are gone.

Collapsed Ducts

A boot is a piece of metal shaped to connect to the round heating duct on one end and to hold the register at the other. In one house, when I put my arm down to check the debris in the duct, I could hardly get my hand into the 4" duct. The flexible duct had been bent so much where it connected to the boot that it had collapsed, restricting the size of the opening. Whoever bought that house would have had a problem balancing his heating system. (I told the builder about it, so presumably it was fixed before the new owners moved in.)

Note that collapsed ducts are not unusual. They shouldn't happen but they do. When you find one, there should be no problem having it fixed.

Master Bedroom Air Return

Consider installing an air return in the master bedroom suite. This serves two purposes. First, when the door of the suite is closed, the flow of air from the registers to the return will not be disrupted. It is not unusual to find that a master bedroom is comfortable when the hall door is open but gets too warm or cool, depending on the time of year, when the door is closed. With a return in the suite, this won't happen.

Second, it keeps a closed door, especially a double door, from rattling every time the furnace goes on or off. When the door is closed and there is no place for the air from the registers to go, the pressure will shove the door hard against the jam. When the furnace fan stops, the pressure is released. The result is a door that can make disturbing noises in the middle of the night. In some cases, this can be helped by putting several little rubber stick-on bumpers on the door jam, the same type that are used on cabinets to keep them from banging. (This isn't a bad idea in any case; it makes it much easier to close a door quietly.)

Thermostats

Several types of thermostats are available. The simplest has a single setting for turning the heater on and off. When you go to bed at night, you turn it down and when you get up in the morning, you turn it up. At the other extreme is a computer-controlled unit that resets the operating temperature several times a day with different settings for weekdays and weekends. As a minimum it is a good idea is to use a unit that includes a clock that lowers and raises the thermostat setting once a day at pre-set times. This will result in a more comfortable house and in savings in heating and air-conditioning operating costs. These are called "set-back" thermostats and are an energy code requirement in California.

If you have trouble setting up your VCR, you should probably avoid the digital units, particularly those that include a lot of functions; they can be tedious to set. It's worthwhile to visit your local heating supply company to get a look at different thermostats.

Location—The thermostat can control the temperature only at one location, so locate the thermostat fairly close to the place whose temperature you want to control most closely. It should not be placed close to a heat register because the furnace will cycle on and off more often than you would want. Since most heat registers are around the exterior of the building, putting thermostats more toward the center of the house usually works best. Normal practice is to put them more-or-less in the flow of air toward a return register.

Thermostats should be installed where average people can see the settings comfortably with little stooping or standing on tip toes.

Seeing Your Thermostat—For a mechanically adjustable thermostat, insist on one which has the setting indicators outside of the box, not inside, and then coordinate the locations of thermostat and lights. If you choose a unit with digital readouts, don't forget that you will need light to see the digital display and you will also need light to see the keyboard when the thermostat is being programmed. (If you put the thermostat in a hall which has closets, don't forget that closets, as well as thermostats, need light. It does take a little coordination effort to get it all right.)

In your specifications spell out the type of thermostat you want and include a proviso that it is to be lighted, either internally or by a light in the hall.

High Efficiency Gas Furnaces

In these days of sensitivity to energy savings, gas furnace manufacturers are offering high efficiency furnaces. Efficiency is used to describe how much of the heat from burning the gas goes into your house and how much goes up the flue. 100 percent efficiencies are not achieved, but some furnaces come surprisingly close (over 95 percent).

An initial installation of a high-efficiency furnace may pay off for you, depending on 1) the cost of gas, 2) the additional cost for the high-efficiency unit, and 3) how much heat you use. It usually takes several years before reduced fuel costs will offset the additional cost of the furnace.

Plumbing

Plumbing plans are less complicated than those used by mechanical subcontractors unless you've included something unusual like circulating hot water. Review plumbing plans to make sure that, when you turn on the water in the shower, there's adequate pipe size so that the water quantity and temperature is only minimally effected by someone washing their hands or flushing a toilet.

Even simple things such as hose bibbs can be user-unfriendly if they're placed inconveniently. If you have plumbing plans, review them to avoid problems.

Look where they may put your hose bibb when you're not looking.

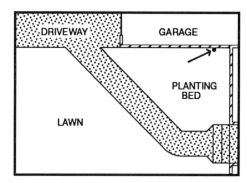

Types of Water Pipe

Copper is the most commonly used pipe inside new houses. However, several types of plastics are available. A discussion of these plastic pipes and their pros and cons is included in Appendix B. You may want to consider one of these for your house. Don't be surprised to find plumbers who know nothing about plastic pipe or who badmouth it. If the Uniform Mechanical Code and/or the building code council in your state has concluded that plastic pipe is okay to use, those conclusions were reached after hearing testimony from many sources including plumbers and suppliers. You can have a reasonable assurance it's okay.

Water Heater Size

Be sure the water heater is suitable for your family. The tendency for builders is to use the smallest (and least expensive) heater allowed by code.

Circulating Hot Water

When your bathroom is a long way from the water heater, you have two options for making hot water quickly available: an auxiliary hot water tank or circulating hot water. The auxiliary hot water tank is discussed in Chapter 9 and instant hot water in Chapter 8.

You are already acquainted with circulating hot water—or did you ever wonder how you got the hot water so fast in your hotel room? The process involves doubling the amount of hot water pipe in the house. One outgoing pipe carries hot water from the heater to the faucets and the other carries cooler water back to the heater. A small pump keeps hot water continuously circulating through the system. Both directions of pipe must be well insulated.

Pay particular attention to keeping the pipe isolated from joists and studs where any noise generated by the continuously running water could be transferred to the wood and amplified by it.

There's an initial cost for putting the system into place and an on-going cost for the electricity to run it. Both costs are relatively small, particularly when you put a timer on the system so that it doesn't run while you sleep.

You can make up at least a part of the cost since you no longer have to waste water by running it until it gets hot. You also get the convenience of having hot water readily available in the kitchen and bathrooms. Consider including the cost of circulating hot water as an option in your specifications so you can decide if it's worthwhile for you. Don't forget, as noted in Appendix B, that some kinds of plastic pipes are not allowed in circulating hot water systems.

Water Pipes in Outside Walls

A good house design will minimize runs of water pipe in the outside walls because of the danger of freezing; for kitchen and vanity sinks, however, short runs of pipe are often located in these walls.

Outside walls in today's new houses are usually well insulated. When water pipes are run in these walls, it is important that the pipes are installed toward the inside of the walls rather than the outside. Also, the wall insulation must be installed so that most of it is between the pipes and the outside wall and only a little, or none, is between the pipes and the inside wall. Plumbers and insulation installers understand this and they normally do it this way. However, it doesn't hurt to check.

Nail Plates

Wallboard is installed on studs using nails or screws that are normally 1¼ to 1½" long and are driven deep into the wallboard. Pipes running through studs or plates are always in danger of being punctured by wallboard fasteners. When the wallboard goes up, the installer can't see where the pipes are. Plumbers put pieces of galvanized sheet metal on the outside of the stud or plate to prevent the wallboard installer from driving a nail or screw there and inadvertently punching a hole in the pipe. These pieces of metal are known as nail plates or safety plates.

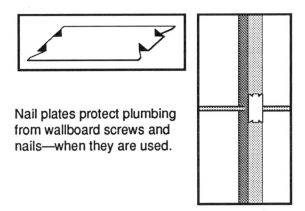

Nail plates protect plumbing from wallboard screws and nails—when they are used.

Noisy Pipes

You can avoid noisy water and drain pipes by paying attention to how the pipes are installed.

Drain water falling from the second-floor of a house makes noticeably more noise in plastic than in iron pipes. If iron pipes are wrapped with insulation, the noise from the second-floor drain pipes will be just about eliminated. However, iron pipe rusts, so check its expected life before installing it. In any case, wrapping with fiberglass insulation will help deaden the noise.

Water running through a pipe is noisier when the pipe touches wood because the wood may act as a sounding board. Generally, water pipe is kept away from wood because running water causes the pipe to vibrate and, if the pipe rubs against wood, the pipe will wear through over time. Plumbers can wrap plastic collars around pipe to protect it, but they don't always do this. You should require that they do. Make sure holes through studs and joists are cut oversized so pipes don't touch wood. If pipes are wrapped with insulation, be sure the plumbers include the insulation through these holes. Find out what the cost for doing this is and include it in your specifications if you can afford it. The house will not sound quite as much like a 1920s hotel when you do.

Hose Bibbs

Hose bibbs are discussed with other outside of the house items in Chapter 11.

Chapter 6

Interiors and Doors

The first part of this chapter discusses interior finishes, wallboard, and moldings; in the second part, we look at interior doors.

Finishes

The trend today is to use light colors and woodwork in homes. This is in sharp contrast to houses constructed even 15 years earlier. Doors and trim may be painted, or natural (stained and lacquered), or a mix of both. It's all up to you. Here are some things to consider when making these decisions.

Walls

Gypsum wallboard is the most commonly used interior wall material. The sheets of board are nailed, glued, and/or screwed to wall studs and ceiling joists. There are gaps where edges of the board meet and irregularities at corners. These are all covered by a thin paper tape and a plaster-like "mud" and made as smooth as the craftsman deems necessary.

Corners may be square or rounded. Generally rounded corners will be a little more costly, but are preferred by most people because of the softer feel they give to a house. It's a matter of personal taste and budget.

Wallpaper

If you plan on having a wall papered, two things are important:

1. Don't let the wallboard people texture the wall. Be sure that someone marks the wall in big red letters to keep this from happening.

2. The corner where the wall meets the ceiling should be straight and even. If the corner is uneven, it is virtually impossible for the wallpaper installer to make the paper look straight across the top of the wall.

Finishing the Wallboard

Wallboard is finished by texturing. This is the process of putting mud on the wall in an uneven pattern. A common finish is called orange peel because of the look of the texture. Ceilings generally have a deeper pattern. Your builder can show you different wallboard textures or you can shop around for the ones you like best.

Building codes require that walls be sealed to make them vapor proof. There are several ways to do this but one is to use a special paint. If you and your builder choose this technique, you'll need to choose your wall colors from among the paints that have this property.

Make sure that the board used on ceilings is designed for ceilings; wallboard should not be used. Ceiling board is stiffer and won't sag between joists.

Baseboard Molding

No Baseboard at All

Builders, when they build houses for someone else, are constrained by their agreement with the buyer or, if it's a spec house, by their estimate of what will sell best. When they build a house for themselves, they are freer to do what they like best. One thing some do is to eliminate baseboard molding in the carpeted areas of the house. This requires that the wallboard be finished all the way to the floor. It also requires the use of hinge-mounted doorstops because there's no molding into which to screw the normal doorstop. And this, in turn, also means that hollow-core doors must be mounted with three hinges, as is explained later.

The carpet covers the area where the wallboard meets the floor, creating a clean, crisp appearance. It's certainly a better looking finish than those seen in most California tract houses which look like they picked up old boards from the scrap heap to use for baseboard moldings. Eliminating baseboard molding also eliminates the problem of getting a good finish on it.

Wooden Baseboard Molding

- In a part of northern California the baseboard moldings are just plain ½" by 3" boards, sometimes with a 45-degree bevel along the top edge and sometimes not. They are painted, not stained. They look cheap and detract significantly from the appearance of the house.

- In other tracts in both northern and southern California builders put in baseboard moldings which are too small, some no bigger than ⅜" × 1½". More than one model was seen where the door slid over the top of a doorstop because there was no place to mount the doorstop high enough to catch the door.

There's no reason you shouldn't have a more decorative molding of reasonable size or to not have any at all.

Rubber Mop Boards

In some houses builders have reverted to an earlier practice of putting rubber mop boards in kitchens, bathrooms, and laundries. Many years ago when a mop consisted of many sloppy twisted pieces of rope-like cotton, rubber mop boards were necessary to protect the bottoms of cupboards from excess mop water. This gave rise to the use of the 3" to 4" rubber mop boards. Today's mops don't do this and wooden baseboards with a reasonable finish are fine. However, if you feel more comfortable with the utilitarian rubber mop boards, they are still available.

Gaps

If the wallboard is not absolutely straight at the bottom, you'll see small but noticeable gaps between the molding and the wallboard. These are particularly visible near outside corners.

If the molding is stained and lacquered, gaps along the baseboard will be clearly visible. They can be fixed but it may involve the wallboard mudder, the finish carpenter, and the painter. And, if the builder has to pay for it, he may argue with you about whether it's necessary.

If you can, check the workmanship after framing and again after wallboard installation to see that the walls are truly straight, at least at the bottom where the molding goes. If the walls aren't straight, insist that the builder have them fixed before the finish carpenter starts work on the baseboards.

When the baseboard molding is painted you have a much better chance of having a finish job that won't draw attention to itself. The finish carpenter or painter can caulk the gaps and paint over them. The imperfections will still be there but will be covered up.

Rounded Wallboard Corners

With rounded corners, there is a problem for the finish carpenter. The molding should follow smoothly around the corner, but this obviously won't happen. The usual solution is to cut a small piece of molding with 45-degree mitered ends and glue it in place across the corners. Gaps will still be noticeable in unpainted molding. but when the molding is painted, the gaps can be caulked and painted, making a more finished appearance.

Small pieces of wood carved to match the baseboard and curved to go around rounded wallboard corners are available, at least for some types of molding. If they can be matched to the molding reasonably well, they may be more attractive than a straight piece at 45 degrees.

With rounded corners and painted moldings, there is still another option; the moldings are simply mitered and cut so that they meet squarely at the corner. This leaves a space between the molding and the rounded wallboard corner. This is filled and painted over. The advantage is the lower cost for the finish carpenter work. The approach is useful only with painted molding although some low-end builders will do the same thing with wood finish moldings by filling the gap and painting it to match the molding.

Vinyl moldings are available in wood-finishes and are used in some low-end houses. If you are trying to save every penny, you may want to take a look at them.

Window Woodwrap

In many parts of the country, window openings are usually encased ('wrapped") in wood. Over 95 percent of the houses in the Pacific Northwest, for example, use woodwrap or offer it as an option. In Arizona, California and other areas with southwestern architecture, the usual approach is to provide a wooden sill or no sill at all; the opening is treated as a continuation of the wallboard. These regional differences can be explained by the weather differences in combination with older single-pane windows. These old windows sweat or wept and woodwrap was needed around the windows in climates with damper, colder winters.

Today's codes require double-pane windows that don't sweat (or at least not much) eliminating the need for woodwrap. Woodwrap has a richer, more finished appearance than does wallboard around a window which is another reason that it has retained its popularity in areas with more traditional architecture.

Woodwrap is an expensive proposition. For example, a tract builder in Tacoma, Washington offered this amenity as an option with a $2000 price tag on it. You might give it some thought, particularly when you plan to paint the wood white against a white wall and then cover it with a valance and drapes so that only the sill shows.

Painted Moldings

Local tradition and custom are strong factors that apply not only to woodwrapped windows but to other decorative wood in the house: baseboard moldings, crown moldings, wainscot, and doors.

Today there is an increasing trend toward painting the woodwork, moldings, woodwrap, and even cabinets and doors. It is the fashionable thing to do. Traditionally, natural wood has been associated with luxury; you painted only when you couldn't afford wood that could be left natural. Or you painted an older house when it was no longer feasible to take care of mars and cracks any other way.

White or near white paint does make a room feel lighter and more open. Too much white may remind you of a doctor's office or a hospital or a service station washroom. A popular compromise is to stain the woodwork a light shade and paint the walls white.

The decision whether to paint or to stain and lacquer is very much one of personal preference. When making it, there's another factor to keep in mind; doors.

Doors

The different types of doors used in today's houses are:

1. Hinged doors. The most common type. Used everywhere, including places they shouldn't be.

2. Sliding glass doors. Used for entering and exiting the house.

3. Sliding wooden doors. Used as closet doors. Sometimes have mirrors.

4. Pocket doors. Used as interior doors where hinged doors would get in the way.

5. Bifold doors. Used primarily for closet doors. May be louvered.

One of the more obvious signs of a poor house design is to find doors that are used inappropriately; hinged doors that should be pocket doors, doors that cover light switches, doors that bang into other doors, doors that block doorways—these and other door-related problems are discussed here.

Exterior Doors

Entry doors are usually decorative and wood is the most popular material. Wood is disadvantageous in three ways: it can warp, finishes deteriorate fairly rapidly when exposed to weather, and it is not a good insulator. If appearance is not a prime consideration, you should consider exterior metal doors. These are a metal sheath over a foam interior. They transmit less heat than wooden doors and have better lasting finishes. Vinyl doors that simulate wood are available. These are also foam filled.

Note that, unlike interior doors discussed below, exterior doors are never hollow core for two reasons:

1. They provide better insulation than do hollow-core doors.

2. Building codes require that solid-core doors be used between the house and the garage because they are better as fire blocks.

Sliding Doors—Exterior doors open inward into houses. In some cases this can cause problems when the room into which the door opens is small. The illustration shows a case where a sliding door would be better.

Entries—Door sidelights have become popular as a way to make entries lighter and more attractive. These narrow vertical panels of glass on one or both sides of the door are often decorative, intended to give the entry a touch of luxury. They also provide an easy way for burglars to break in and unlock the door. (Security is discussed in more detail in Appendix M.)

Unless planned carefully, sidelights can cause problems with light switch location. Without the sidelights the switch box would go right where one of the sidelights is located. The entry door is

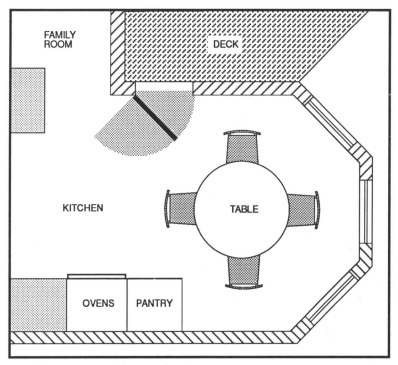

A sliding door wouldn't get in the way.

Entry door side-
lights are attractive.
They also make it
easy for burglars.

always in a load-bearing wall. Framers tend to fill the area around the door and the sidelights with studs, leaving no place for the switches. This should all be figured out ahead of time.

With all of the framing lumber, the switches could not be placed next to the door where they belong.

Another sometimes-heard objection to entry door sidelights is that someone can see into the house. The windows are so small that putting an attractive blind or curtain over them is difficult but, without something, you lose your privacy at night. To let light in during the day while avoiding this fish-bowl aspect of door sidelights, some builders use glass bricks or acrylic blocks instead of window panes. You may want to give some thought to the advantages of using other than transparent sidelights.

Interior Doors

Since insulation value and security are of no relevance, interior doors are chosen for their appearance.

Interior doors are usually hollow core although solid-core doors are sometimes seen. In a hollow core door a veneer of wood, molded hardboard, or vinyl covers a frame of wood that goes around the outside of the door and across the center. The center piece is used to mount the door latch. The rest of the interior of the door has a honeycomb of material to give support to the veneer on the outside.

Interior doors may be painted or finished to match the woodwork in the house. They may be a raised-panel design or a single solid surface. The single surface doors are usually a hardwood veneer intended for staining and lacquer or varnish. Raised panel doors come in several different styles in wood and simulated-wood hard-board or vinyl surfaces.

White hardboard with white painted molding is a common finish although some builders choose a mixture of white doors and natural woodwork and vice-versa. The white hardboard raised-panel doors can be painted or finished to look stained.

Bifold Doors—Bifold doors are often used in preference to sliding or hinged doors, particularly for closets. They have advantages and disadvantages.

Bifold doors always block part of the entry and can be a real annoyance when installed in closets that aren't walk-in. A disturbing characteristic of double bifold doors is that when you close one side the other side pops open. This is usually because the hardware wasn't adjusted properly. Also, as you close one door, air pressure builds up in the closet which forces the other door to open. Louvered bifolds can alleviate this problem.

Some designs in starter homes have the laundry room just off of the kitchen with bifold doors to close off the laundry. You'll have a serious noise problem unless sound insulation is used around the laundry and the door closes snugly. Louvered doors cannot shut out the sound and are a poor choice for a laundry.

Bifold closet doors sometimes have full-length mirrors mounted on them. Hardware for bifold doors is not designed for the weight of the mirrors, resulting in doors that seem rickety when they are opened or closed.

Pocket Doors—Pocket doors need different considerations. The pocket must be deep enough for the door to be pushed all the way in. Nothing else can go into the wall where the pocket is—no wiring, outlets, switches, or plumbing. Sometimes the pocket door may not be possible even when it otherwise makes the most sense.

Any place where a hinged door would be in the way when left open is a good place for a pocket door. Walk-in closets are good examples. You want a door you can close, but you don't want one you have to close from the inside to get to your clothes. (Hinged doors are obviously okay when they don't get in the way when open.) The door into the toilet/bath part of a master bedroom suite is another place where a pocket door may be better. Still another is a walk-in pantry.

Hinged doors are frequently used between dining rooms and kitchens. They shouldn't because when open, they take valuable wall space if swung into the dining room or block counters if swung into the kitchen. They can also interfere with refrigerators. A pocket door, or even no door at all, is preferable.

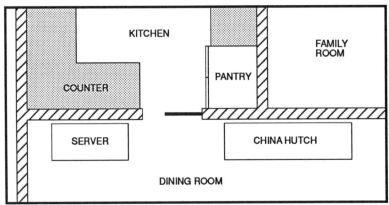

A pocket door (or no door at all) is the user-friendly solution between the kitchen and the dining room

Look at your floor plan carefully to see where pocket doors should be used rather than hinged doors. Replacing a hinged door with a pocket door on a floor plan may not be easy when the walls beside the hinged door mount the room light switch, an outlet, or contain water pipes (like to a shower head). It may take some rearranging to use the pocket door, such as putting the shower head at the other end of the shower, moving the light switch to the other side of the doorway, etc. If you can eliminate an inappropriate hinged door, however, it will be worth it.

- Pocket doors are not always the favorite things for workers. Like the carpenter who mounted the paper holder in the bathroom but had forgotten that there was a pocket door in the wall. And there was the building designer who got a call from the electrician wiring a house to say that there was a pocket door in the wall where the designer had shown an outlet in the house design. Caveat emptor!

Doorstops

While visiting Tracy, California, I saw a new house with a small guest closet off the entry. As is customary there, the closet has a hollow core door mounted by two hinges. The doorstop is the style that mounts on a hinge. Within a week after the buyers moved in, a gust of wind caught the door and the doorstop punched a hole through the thin veneer of the door. Someone should have been more careful. But who?

Not the home user. The builder screwed up. Our house has the same kind of doors and doorstops. But we'll never have this problem because our doors are all mounted with three hinges, not two, and stops are on the center hinges.

The carpenter and the builder should have known that the only place with any strength in a hollow-core door is across the door center. Inside the door at that point is a block of wood (the rail) for mounting the door latch. When a door is mounted with three hinges, and the center hinge is used for the doorstop, the stop hits the door over this block. When the stop is placed on the top or bottom hinge where there is no block inside of the door, the stop can make a hole in the thin veneer.

Often, these kinds of doorstops are put on upside down. There is a right and a wrong way. When it's installed the right way, the stop hits the door and the door trim squarely but, when they are wrong, they hit at an angle.

It is good practice to use hinge-mounted doorstops only where there is no alternative because they are much more likely to cause damage to hinges.

Doors Banging into Doors

• In a neighbor's new home a downstairs half-bath and a closet open off opposite sides of a short hall. The original floor plan called for the door into the half-bath to be a pocket door. The buyer wanted a hinged door instead. This door and the hall closet door now occupy the same hall space when open. The bathroom door could have been installed to open on the other side but it wasn't. The builder could have taken the time to look at the door arrangements. He didn't. The carpenter did his thing and the home user is living with yet another irritation.

Another example is a front entry door swinging in front of the entry closet door. This arrangement can be inconvenient at times.

- A model in Modesto, California has a single hinged door between the master bedroom and the bath/vanity area. When opened, this door swings right across the doorway into the walk-in closet. From the bedroom you have go into the bath/vanity area and then close the door you just came through before you can get into the closet. Not a good arrangement.

- In a custom house design in Tigard, Oregon, the door from the master bedroom into the bathroom opens right across the door into the room where the toilet is. So to get to the toilet, you must go from the bedroom into the bathroom, then close the door you just came through so you can open the door to get to the toilet. Wanna' try this in the middle of the night?

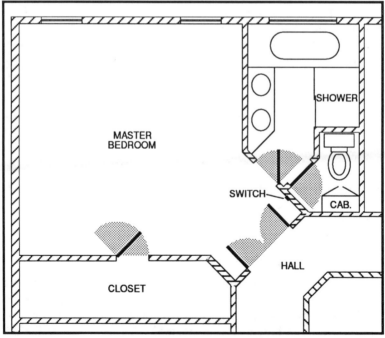

An unfortunate master bedroom design: One door blocks another, the switch is behind a double door, and the closet should have a pocket door.

Double Doors

Designers and builders use double doors as entries into houses, master bedrooms, and dens to give a touch of luxury to a floor plan. After all, if your house is big enough to use double doors then it's obviously in the luxury class. Well, maybe.

The location of light switches is a particular problem with double doors. When you have to take more than one step to reach a light switch after entering the room through a double door, you need a better arrangement. The actual placement of light switches for double doors was discussed in Chapter 4. They should never be behind a door.

The light switch is most accessible when it's on the wall just past the end of the door normally used for going in and out. Therefore, be sure that the drawings show which door will normally be used as the entry and which will be fixed.

Doors and Furniture

Double doors, when opened, sometimes occupy wall space where you intended to place furniture.

- My Oregon home had double doors between the master bedroom and the vanity area. The designer's floor plan showed these doors opening into the vanity area—one door blocking the doorway into the toilet/shower room and the other door blocking light

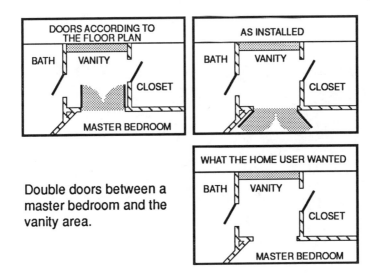

Double doors between a master bedroom and the vanity area.

switches. The carpenter noticed this and decided that the doors should swing into the bedroom—where they blocked two walls from having furniture on them. After living in the house for several months I removed both doors, leaving a totally acceptable archway and a much less irritated wife.

The problem with double doors interfering with furniture placement also occurs with single doors.

Sometimes the solution may be a pocket door, as mentioned earlier; in other cases simply hinging the door from the other side may solve the problem. At times you may be forced to accept a compromise in door location. Take a good look at your floor plan to prevent door problems before your house is built.

Doors and Stairs

In several houses well above the starter-house price range, the entry door, when open, blocks the stairway. It is awkward; it can be lived with. It would be better if it weren't that way.

Chapter 7

Other Whole-House Considerations

This chapter concludes the discussion of the items which involve the whole house rather than a single room or area.

Windows

In Arizona and California there is usually lots of glass in the houses, a little less elsewhere. Where summers are hot, it's a good idea to be able to block out the sun in south- and west-facing windows. Not only does this reduce the load on the air conditioner but it also reduces the amount of fading the sun can cause to furniture and carpets. As a first step, tinting the windows with a plastic sheet will help. It's usually not enough.

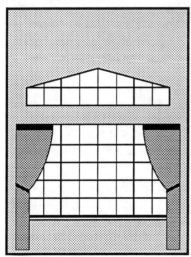 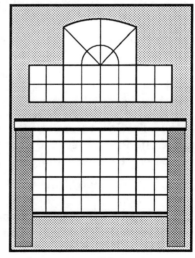

Windows high on walls are often serious sun problems because they are hard to decorate.

The biggest problems occur on walls that are two stories tall like those found in many homes with southwestern architecture. To maintain a feeling of airiness, windows are often placed above the normal ones. The additional upper windows are usually rectangular but aren't as wide as the lower windows. They may also be triangular, round, half round, or some combination of these. In all cases they are hard to decorate with coverings that open and close—an important feature for south- and west-facing windows.

Decorating Problems

Small round windows high up on a wall are used to break up the expanse of the wall. Because there is no satisfactory way to decorate them, such windows are usually left alone, letting the sun do its thing. Shades are available for half-round fan-light windows, but they can be expensive. If you plan on using woodwrap on windows, be aware that windows with curved shapes are a headache for the craftsman.

Another hard-to-decorate situation is found in bay windows in which the ceiling of the bay is low, with only a couple of inches between the window and the ceiling. Any kind of valance will block part of the glass.

In the warmer climates of the southwest, tall walls make it impossible for roof overhangs to provide shade for windows. This is something most people don't consider when selecting a house plan and/or situating the house on the lot.

When choosing the windows for your house, always remember the exposure; on the south and west sides of the house, you'll want windows that will let you keep the hot summer sun out.

Double Pane Windows

In the following discussion we use the term "double pane." Those in the building trades tend to say "double glazed." For our purposes they're the same thing.

The size and shape of the windows are controlled by the house plans, but you still have to make some decisions. First, if you live in an area where double-pane windows aren't a code requirement, you have to decide whether to pay the extra money for them. I suggest you do because of the saving in energy consumption and because of the greater comfort they provide. It's also nice to not have to be concerned about windows that sweat or weep.

Double-pane windows are made with or without a decorative grid between the panes. This grid makes the windows appear to be made up of a number of pieces of glass when, in fact, they are not. More and more of these windows use vinyl-clad frames for its better insulation. The vinyl is usually white but other colors are available. (Any color other than white can limit your choice of house colors.)

You will also have to decide whether the windows will open and, if they do, how. Your choices include vertical (sash) windows, horizontal sliding windows, and casement windows. An interior decorator noted that casement windows sometimes cause problems because the handles keep drapes and mini-blinds from falling cleanly to the window sill. Using knobs, rather than handles for opening and closing the windows, helps this problem but causes difficulties for people who have trouble grasping with their hands.

In states where energy conservation has become an important part of building codes, windows are a special problem. In most houses, windows account for more heat transfer between inside and outside than walls, floors, ceilings, or doors. Some codes restrict the amount of glass, including skylights, you can put in your house. Appendix B includes a discussion of energy codes for the three Pacific coast states. If you live in an area where you are restricted by the amount of glass you are allowed, you obviously cannot choose certain floor plans.

In any case, be aware that the greater the amount of glass, the greater your heating and cooling bills. Also, where energy codes are in effect, the older single pane windows are no longer allowed and the cost of windows is significantly higher than it used to be. Thus they become more of a cost factor in choosing your floor plan.

Skylights

Most of today's house designs include skylights. They are used in place of windows where windows would be inconvenient (as in small bathrooms), where windows aren't possible (as in an interior room which has no outside wall), or where they let in light while still maintaining privacy. There are penalties to pay when skylights are used. Like windows, they are poor insulators. In general, it's not possible to shade them from the hot afternoon sun. When this is a problem, skylights will need to be made from tinted glass or they'll need some kind of interior blinds.

Where skylights are used in rooms like bathrooms which do not use vaulted ceilings, there is a shaft or 'well' that brings the light down from the roof-mounted skylight. This well is often tapered so that it is bigger at the bottom than the top thus spreading the light over a bigger area in the room.

Skylights range from one to four feet on a side. Think carefully before using the smaller sizes. Many people don't like their appearance, feeling they look cheap.

Closets

If building designers spent as many hours doing housework in the houses they design as they spend in designing them, there are some things they'd be quick to change. Closet design is one of them.

Walk-in Closets

In the Pacific Northwest the most commonly used doors for walk-in closets are hinged. These should not open into a closet in such a way that the door blocks access to any of the closet's interior. Apparently this is easier to say than do considering the large number of closets built this way. In a recent Tour of Homes in Salem, Oregon, 30 houses had master bedroom walk-in closets with hinged closet doors, and in 40 percent of those the door blocked some part of the interior when open.

Closets and Accessibility

Most closets that use sliding, hinged, or bifold doors are designed to make them partly inaccessible! It's probably not deliberate but it's not user-friendly either. The problem is that the front openings of the closets are too narrow. It's not unusual to see closets with over a foot of closet past the end of the door opening.

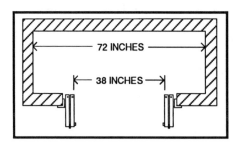

When closet doors are not as wide as the closet, they severely limit access.

Add 6 or 7 inches of a folded bifold door in the front of the opening and you can have close to 18 inches of inaccessible closet on at least one end. Try getting a coat or dress out of the end of that closet and you'll be more than a little annoyed.

Closet Interiors

It used to be that a closet had just a shelf and a pole for hanging clothes. Some still do but other, more useful, arrangements are seen in today's houses. These include built-in shelves for shoes or whatever else the home user may want. Poles may be two levels in height for greater utility.

Some builders use stiff vinyl-coated steel wire instead of shelves in closets. Again, these may or may not appeal to you.

Here's a little problem, easy to fix when it arises, but annoying when it happens to every clothes rod in every closet in your house. In less than two years in our new house we've had clothes dumped on the floor seven times by the pole sockets breaking. Pole sockets are the plastic, wood, or metal pieces which hold the ends of the clothes rods or poles. Ours were a translucent white plastic that, over a short period of time, de-plasticized, lost their strength and just simply split in two. If you find these in your house, keep your fingers crossed. If the first one breaks, bite the bullet and replace them all because it'll be just a matter of time until the rest go. (We've gone over to wooden sockets which won't de-plasticize.) If you take care of this in your specifications, the problem won't arise.

Plastic pole sockets don't last: before and after less than a year.

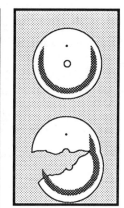

Floors

The common materials used for floors are carpet, linoleum, hardwood, tile, marble, and field stone. With all of these it usually doesn't pay to buy the cheapest thing around. It simply won't last.

Subfloors

If you choose hardwood flooring that has to be nailed down, make sure it's nailed to plywood rather than particle board. Particle board won't hold nails and the flooring will loosen with usage.

Unless special precautions are taken, unyielding materials, like ceramic tile, marble, and other stone, will come loose or crack. These materials should be laid on a very solid base. Most subfloors don't meet this requirement. With post-and-beam construction and its 2" deck under the flooring, the deck lumber can be expected to dry out, warping in the process. Further, changes in temperature and humidity will cause the boards to move.

Floor joists made of sawn or dimensioned lumber are subject to the same drying and warping. Composite ('silent floor') joists are more stable over time but are still subject to changes in temperature and humidity. Slab floors, of course, won't shift but they can develop hairline cracks which can cause the tile above it to crack if the tile is rigidly attached to the slab.

To get the necessary rigidity, special treatment under ceramic tile or stone should be used. This may consist of a concrete-like foundation or mud, thick plywood, or backer board made of concrete mortar with fiberglass mesh reinforcing. Ceramic tile should not be laid on particle board or interior grade plywood, because it's not stable with changes in humidity.

To get the required stiffness with plywood, it should be exterior grade measuring at least ¾" thick. Backer boards are typically ⅜" or ⁷⁄₁₆" thick and make better backers. You should specify that backer board is to be used under floors of tile or stone.

Tile Entry Ways

Ceramic tile entry ways can cause accidents when someone with wet shoes comes into the house. The glaze on a lot of tile is smooth which gets slippery when wet. Tiles made for entries should be either unglazed or have a texture to reduce their slickness.

To test a tile's suitability for your entry way, take a pair of rubber-soled shoes, put some water on the tile, and test the traction. The people at the tile store can advise you on the best purchase.

Squeaky Floors

Squeaky floors are a source of irritation. Oftentimes there's little that can be done about them—not, at least, at a reasonable cost. They are a real turn off for potential buyers.

Particle board is usually used under carpeting. It has the characteristic of changing size with temperature and humidity so if it is laid without adequate space between pieces, it can cause squeaks when pieces expand and rub together. This is something which is hard to write into specifications but, if you see it when the house is being built, don't hesitate to speak up.

Squeaky floors can develop as the lumber in a house dries out. Usually, lumber shrinks or warps with time, leaving a gap between the beam or floor joist and the deck or subfloor just above it. When someone walks on it, the floor or subfloor will give and move up and down on its nails. This rubbing on the nails can cause squeaks.

This doesn't usually happen until the house is one to two years old. Then you're on your own unless you have an agreement with the builder that he's responsible for more than the year of the normal move-in warranty. The best insurance is to take all the reasonable steps you can to eliminate the sources of the squeaks during house construction.

- You don't want to become like a neighbor who, after about 9 months in his new house, couldn't walk in his bedroom or dining room without causing a squeak. In his case the problem was covered by his 1-year warranty. The carpet had to be taken out and the subfloor nailed down. A few months later and any squeak fixing would have been on the owner's nickel, not the builder's.

Not all floors will have squeaks. With slab floors, for example, there's nothing to squeak. There are different squeak mechanisms for post-and-beam construction than for floors that use joists.

With Post and Beam

This is the most common crawl-space construction used in the western states. Typically four-inch wide beams are spaced on 4-foot centers and are supported every eight feet by posts that rest on concrete piers under the house. Two-inch lumber, typically 2" × 8", is then laid across the beams to form a deck on which the house is built. A plywood, particle-board, or tile backer-board surface is laid on the deck as the subflooring onto which the carpet, linoleum, or other flooring surface is laid.

There are a number of places where squeaks can develop. An obvious place is where the deck is nailed to the beams. As the beams dry and warp, or as the deck lumber warps, nails will pull up and then squeak when someone walks on them. The deck lumber warping can cause the subflooring nails to pull loose, another place for squeaks. Since it is unreasonable to assume that dried lumber will be used, the best bet is to do the best possible job of fastening the deck pieces down, using screws or lots and lots of nails.

With Floor Joists

Some construction uses floor joists with much longer spans than are feasible with beams. Joists are used on second floors, in houses with basements, and in other places as an alternative to concrete piers and posts. Joists may be either sawn lumber or they may be manufactured joists made like I beams in which multiple pieces of wood are glued together to form joists. These are lighter, stronger, and longer than a single piece of sawn lumber. As the price of sawn lumber increases, these manufactured joists are becoming price competitive. Joists are typically installed on 16" centers and plywood is laid across them as the subfloor. Gluing the subfloor to the joists eliminates one possible source of squeaks.

These manufactured joists are advertised as the way to have a silent floor. Since they're made with dried wood, as is the plywood on top of them, there's nothing to dry out and warp, hence nothing to cause squeaks. Unfortunately there are other sources of squeaks with these floors. Joists are held in place with specially-shaped metal hangers. If the joists are not properly fastened to the hangers then walking on the floor above can cause the joist to move in the hanger, causing a squeak.

Talk to your builder about the use of silent joists vs. those made with sawn lumber. Where the span is long, the manufactured joists may be the only choice. If manufactured joists are not used, then consider having the subfloor fastened down with screws rather than nails.

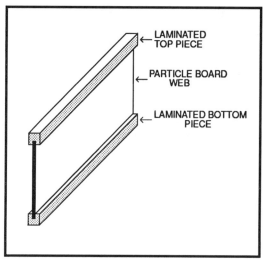

A 1.5" × 12" 'silent floor' joist.

Fireplaces

Most floor plans include a fireplace. Appendix E discusses the different kinds of fireplaces used and their pros and cons. As explained there, gas fireplaces are not presently allowed by code in California although inefficient gas logs are.

If you live where gas fireplaces are allowed, consider the following:

- Top vent gas fireplaces waste room heat up the vent pipe continuously, whether lit or not.

- Direct vent gas fireplaces do not have this characteristic and are preferable.

- Ventless gas fireplaces dump their burned gasses directly back into the room, an arrangement which is not recommended in today's tight houses.

Ceilings

In many of today's two-story houses, the living and dining rooms are two-stories tall and many one-story houses have vaulted ceilings for the two rooms. These ceilings are all high and give a feeling of airiness. But watch out for ceilings in other rooms. Large rooms need high ceilings or they will seem oppressive.

- One house in Salem, Oregon is on a hillside lot with a nice view of the city. The great room has a ceiling that is 7-feet 9-inches high. It has a feeling of being even less than that. It is oppressive. The builder had trouble selling the house. That low ceiling in a big room was a real turnoff.

Note that "8-foot" ceilings are frequently a few inches lower than this. Builders do this to save on studs which come in 8' and 10' lengths. In order to use the 8' piece, the inside of the room is made smaller.

Attic Storage

If you plan on having attic storage, then:

- Specify that the attic area is to be stick framed or that special attic trusses are used to leave a maximum of open area in the attic.

- Specify that any attic insulation should be roll or batting.

- Specify how much and what type of attic flooring is used.

- Specify the means of access you want, such as a door off of an upstairs hall or bedroom or a pull-down ladder in the garage.

- Screw-in bare-light sockets mounted to a ceiling rafter are entirely adequate for attic lighting and should be specified. A switch for actuating the lights should be mounted at the entry to the storage area.

Quiet Please!

- When we bought our new house, we didn't notice that the location for the entertainment center in the family room would be just a 4-inch wall away from the head of the bed in the master bedroom. Going to bed early means using ear plugs.

While it's possible to insulate the walls after construction, it would have been much better to have it done before. Optimal sound insulation can be installed when the house is built but not after the wallboard is in place.

It's a good idea to put sound insulation in the walls around bathrooms so that you or your guests are not awakened by early risers or middle-of-the-night users.

Laundry room walls are good places for sound insulation, especially if they're next to the living area of the house, particularly the eating area, den, or bedroom.

Sound insulation is relatively inexpensive to install before wallboard is put in place. It's far better to think ahead than to consider a retrofit.

Security

Security issues discussed in Appendix M include entry door styles, methods of securing doors, fire safety, security lights, garage door openers, garage sidedoors, and alarm systems. Many of these items are not expensive to have done in a more secure fashion when this is important to you.

Part III

The Parts of
the House

Kitchen
Bedrooms
Baths
Entry
Halls
Stairs
Dining Room
Family Room
Laundry
Garage
Exterior Materials
Roofs
Concrete
Under the House
Hose Bibbs

Chapter 8

The Kitchen

Because of the amount of time a family spends in the kitchen, it is the room which should be scrutinized most carefully. Unfortunately, it is also the room where more user-unfriendly things are done than in any other. In this chapter we look at ways to make a kitchen better and friendlier.

Kitchen Layout

Small kitchens make for few steps but don't have enough counter and cabinet space to make them easy to use. Larger kitchens require more steps but they can be more user-friendly and result in less overall work. The size of the kitchen is a compromise between these two aspects. Whatever its size, the layout itself involves a number of different considerations.

First and foremost, the kitchen should be an **easy** place to work. The work area should not be a traffic path from one room to another or from outside the house to the rest of the house. Whoever is working in the kitchen doesn't need to have people in the way when food is being prepared or cleanup is under way.

Traditionally the kitchen work area has been designed as a triangle with the stove, sink, and refrigerator at the corners. However, today's homes have four amenities that weren't found in the kitchens when this triangle idea evolved: 1) stoves with the cooktop and ovens separated, 2) dishwashers, 3) microwave ovens and 4), in many houses, islands.

To reduce the steps used in the preparation of and cleanup after a meal, the areas involved should be close together. There should be room for two people—after all, anyone can use a little help.

There should be work areas, i.e., counter spaces, in the right places and they should be good-sized. You should have places around the stove and refrigerator to set things. With these thoughts in mind, the following guidelines are offered. The first five items are explained in detail below:

1. The dishwasher should be adjacent to the sink.

2. There should be ample counter workspace next to the kitchen sink.

3. There should be counter space in front of the refrigerator for setting things.

4. Refrigerators should be placed so that doors can open fully and so that extra steps are not needed to walk around them.

5. Islands in kitchens should not cause extra steps to get around and shouldn't cause congestion.

6. Cabinets for storing dishes should be close to the dishwasher.

7. Cabinets for storing pots and pans should be close to the cooktop.

8. There should be counter space next to the cooktop where hot pans, cooking ingredients, and/or serving dishes can be set.

9. There should be counter space next to ovens where hot things can be placed.

10. Cooktops can be separated from the refrigerator since rarely does food go directly from one to the other.

11. Ovens can be separated from the refrigerator for the same reason.

12. If possible, the shape and size of the kitchen should be such that the floor can be covered with a single piece of linoleum rather than needing a seam.

Dishwashers Should Always Be Adjacent to the Sink.

Dishes usually need to be cleaned off and rinsed before going into the dishwasher. You don't need space between the sink and the dishwasher where rinsed dishes or silverware can drip on the floor. Unfortunately, this design flaw is common in many homes, even the most expensive ones.

The dishwasher should never be in a counter which is at right angles to the sink because this leaves a space where water can drip between the counter and the open dishwasher door.

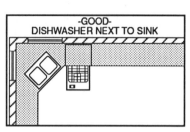

There are good and bad arrangements for the sink and the dishwasher.

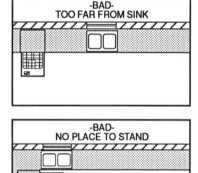

A fairly popular option is to put the sink in a corner at a 45-degree angle and the dishwasher under one of the adjacent counters. If there is only one door under the sink, hinge that door on the same side as the dishwasher. Otherwise the door can't be opened when the dishwasher is open.

Another thing to watch for is a dishwasher which, when open, blocks a passageway to another part of the kitchen.

Counter Workspace

Workspace should be provided adjacent to the kitchen sink since that's where the preparation of food for the stove, for serving, or for storing in the refrigerator usually takes place. This workspace is desirable because its proximity to the sink makes it easy to clean up.

It's also where space is needed for dirty dishes, glassware, and pots and pans before they're readied for the dishwasher.

Distances from this work space to the cooktop, ovens, pantry, and refrigerator are important. This is where you save steps.

Refrigerator Placement

Appendix C is a detailed discussion about refrigerators, their sizes and their door arrangements. It explains the reasons for the recommendations made here.

To have counter space in front of the refrigerator will mean that the refrigerator will have to be across a fairly narrow passage (3½ to 4 feet) from a counter. This can be a peninsula or an island as well as the end of a counter.

- A refrigerator should never be placed against a wall on either side which is deeper than the body of the refrigerator, exclusive of the doors.

- A refrigerator should never be placed against a wall which has a door at the front of the refrigerator.

- A refrigerator should never be placed where it is necessary to walk around one of its doors to reach a counter to set things on.

- The side of a refrigerator should never be placed against a counter which does not face the same way as the refrigerator.

There should always be a counter directly in front of the refrigerator.

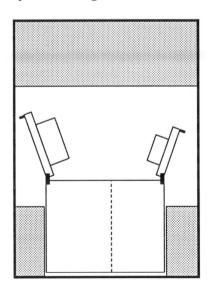

When laying out a kitchen or looking at an existing one, remember that, except for the smallest of refrigerators, the unit will stick out 9 to 12 inches farther than the adjacent counter, cupboard, or pantry. (Also remember this when looking at floor plans. Most of them are very inaccurate in this regard.)

Be sure that the opening for the refrigerator is big enough. For 20 to 27 cu. ft. units consider the following dimensions:

• Heights run from about 67 to 71 inches,
• Widths from 31 to 36 inches,
• Body depths (exclusive of doors) 27 to 29 inches, and
• Overall depths from 31 to 35 inches.

And don't forget that a couple of inches are necessary behind the unit to connect the water for the ice maker and for the electrical plug.

The opening should be large enough to make it reasonably easy to roll the unit in and out of its niche. Allow at least an inch on each side and two inches on the top of the unit for this.

When considering a kitchen design, take time to measure your refrigerator and be sure it will fit. Also don't forget that even though yours is okay today, sometime you are likely to replace it and usually with a bigger unit. You want room to do that. And, of course, there's the ever-present concern about the people who will be buying your house someday and the size of the refrigerator they may have.

One last consideration: the connection for the water for the ice maker should be recessed into the wall. One developer in Castaic, California did not do this. There may be more. This adds another couple of inches of useless space behind the refrigerator.

Peninsulas and Islands

Islands and peninsulas are frequently used to separate the kitchen from the adjacent family room.

Islands or peninsulas may be used to house a stove or sink, or to provide counter and cabinet space. Some designs use an island to house a TV set which faces into the adjacent family room. Peninsulas and islands are also used as eating bars.

For islands to really work, the kitchen must be large enough to leave room between the island and counters, cabinets, and the refrigerator so that the whole area isn't crowded.

- In one kitchen in Tracy, California, there is less than three feet between the back of the island and the refrigerator. That means you can't get the door fully open on a large freezer-over model refrigerator.

  The space between the end of the island and the counter with the dishwasher is 32 inches. When the dishwasher door is open it's necessary to go around the island to get to the other side of the dishwasher. Two people can't work in the kitchen because the island is in the way.

Before choosing a plan that has a cooktop mounted in a peninsula or an island, consider the impact on the kitchen exhaust system. (See Appendix I for a discussion of these systems.)

Exhaust systems need a duct and there must be a place to run it. This can have an impact on the cabinet design if the cabinets are needed to cover the duct after it exits from the hood or microwave oven.

An island cooktop requires a down-draft exhaust system which is not as effective as an up-draft system, is noisier, and is more expensive. From the point of view of having an effective exhaust system, an island cooktop is not the way to go. There can also be lighting problems as discussed next.

Lighting

General Kitchen Lighting

In California and Arizona, fluorescent panels are common; in some places such as the Pacific Northwest, you frequently find multiple can or flood lights. Choose what you want but make sure you have enough light in the kitchen.

- An attractive scheme was seen in one house in Salem, Oregon. In the center of the large kitchen was a decorative translucent panel with a skylight above it. At night, fluorescent lights mounted in the well of the skylight give the illusion of daylight.

Light for the Cooktop

If you use an island down-draft exhaust system, check that there is good lighting for the cooktop. Usually there is no special light for the island unless you ask for it. Sometimes a skylight is used to provide light during the day, but night can be another problem.

Light for the Sink

Light for the kitchen sink is usually as simple as putting a light over the sink when the house is built. One attractive, but different, arrangement was seen in a model house in Carlsbad, California. It has a problem you'll want to avoid:

• The sink is in front of a large window that goes to the ceiling. The ceiling has skylights that come down to the tops of the windows, giving a solarium effect. During the day, all that light and airiness is appealing. At night, however, there is no provision for lighting the sink and surrounding countertop.

If you run across this arrangement in a house design, be sure you figure out a way to get light into the sink or forget the design. If you want to use this arrangement anyway, consider the orientation of the kitchen relative to the sun, because it will be a problem for south or west facing kitchens.

Most houses have a window in front of the sink. Large windows make the kitchen feel more open but take away wall space that might be better used for cabinets.

The Breakfast Nook

Light in the breakfast nook is usually provided by a small chandelier or some kind of hanging fixture. If you prefer, a ceiling fan can be used in place of the chandelier. For this reason, when the chandelier is installed, have its mounting made strong enough for a ceiling fan. Have a 3-wire cable run to the switch location. Depending on the exact layout of the nook, be careful about the placement of the overhead fixture. If you're not, you may find that the chandelier isn't centered over the table, and it may not be that easy to change. Chandeliers can be swagged but ceiling fans present more of a problem to move.

(A "swagged" ceiling fixture is one where the electrical box is mounted in one place and the fixture hangs from another. A loop of wire and chain, the swag, is then necessary between the electrical box and the top of the chain holding the fixture.)

A Salem, Oregon builder solved the question of where to put the chandelier by lighting the nook with can lights. This is okay as long as no one ever wants a ceiling fan. Just make sure there are **enough** lights (which this builder didn't do.)

The Kitchen Sink

Here are some user-friendly features you may want to look for when considering the kitchen sink:

1. A sink that's level with or recessed below the countertop is more user-friendly than one with a lip (which gets in the way when cleaning up in the kitchen.) Note that counter-level or recessed sinks are not available with plastic laminate countertops.

2. If you choose a sink that is divided into two uneven parts, think about where you want the narrow part, which usually contains the disposal. The consideration here is the location of the dishwasher and whether you want the disposal next to the dishwasher or not. In any case, you should decide whether the disposal should be on the same side of the sink as the dishwasher.

3. You may want a sink which has extra holes along the back apron of the sink. These holes could be for instant hot water, filtered water, for a hose with a sprayer for rinsing dishes, and/or for a soap dispenser.

Outlet Under the Kitchen Sink

A split-wired dual outlet is usually placed in the back wall under the kitchen sink. One side of the outlet is wired to the garbage disposal's on-off switch and the other side of the outlet is hot all the time. In some areas, the hot side of the outlet is used to power the dishwasher and in others the dishwasher is not plugged into an outlet but is wired permanently to the house wiring. This leaves the hot half of the outlet available for an instant hot water unit.

In some areas the practice is to not put any outlet under the sink at all. The disposal and the dishwasher are permanently wired in place. If any work has to be done on them or if they must be replaced, it requires both an electrician and a plumber.

Instant Hot Water

After you've been in the house a while and you run gallons and gallons of water down the drain several times a day before hot water reaches the kitchen from the water heater, you decide that in these days of water shortages it would be not only convenient but also socially responsible to install an instant hot water unit. But look what's involved when there is no outlet.

You may think it shouldn't be too tough to drill a hole through the cabinet wall and connect your instant hot water unit to the dishwasher's power. Ha! The dishwasher takes 15 amperes and is on a 15A or 20A circuit. If you add the instant hot water unit (about 6 amperes), you'll overload the circuit.

So insist that a non-switched outlet be put under the sink and, if the local practice is to plug the dishwasher into an outlet, get a separate one for the instant hot water.

Kitchen or Family Room?

In today's open floor plans the family room and kitchen are often more like one room than two.

You might encounter a potential floor covering problem when a peninsula or island eating bar separates the kitchen and family room. Many builders put the family room carpeting all the way to the bar. Food and drink spills can ruin your carpet, so you might want to consider linoleum in that area.

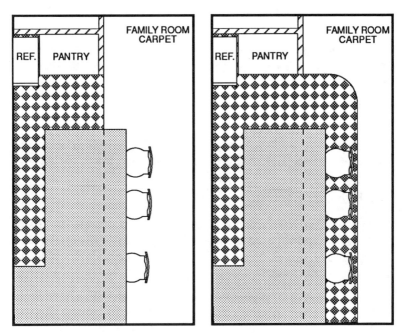

Carpet doesn't belong under the breakfast bar.

Appliances

The configuration of the stove's cooktop and oven or ovens are decided as a part of the house design. You will need to decide if the stove is to operate with gas or electricity and then select manufacturers and model numbers.

Similarly, you need to choose the disposal, dishwasher, and built-in microwave oven, if applicable.

This information is used for pricing and for the design of the cabinets. All the units, except the disposal, need to have the cabinetry designed around them. Be sure to specify how high you want the ovens, both thermal and microwave, above the floor because these dimensions vary widely from one builder to another.

Thermal Ovens

The height of thermal ovens should not make it difficult for a short person to get a hot roasting pan out of an oven.

- This seems obvious, but there are tract models in Carlsbad, California where the two thermal ovens are so high that it would take a professional basketball player to use them.

  The models were made by a large, well-known company which builds for the middle to upper price range. Reputation isn't everything—you still have to keep a Buyer Beware attitude.

Microwave Ovens

Watch carefully the height of microwave ovens installed above a cooktop. Place the microwave oven about 21" above the cooktop so it's out of the way and so shorter people can see into it easier.

The Exhaust System

Review Appendix I, which includes a detailed discussion of updraft and downdraft exhaust systems. They are not all equal in collecting smoke, fumes, etc., and they are not all equal in getting rid of what they do collect.

The most effective arrangement is an updraft unit with a hood large enough to cover all the cooktop. Units that mount the fan in the attic area will be less noisy than those with the fan in the hood itself.

Ductless exhaust systems for downdraft, updraft, or microwave ovens are ineffective. Do not choose a downdraft unit for other than an island installation; they're noisier and less effective than updraft systems.

If the presence of the hood is aesthetically unappealing to you, you can use a hood that pulls out when you need it but doesn't stick out past the surrounding cabinets when not in use. These are described in the appendix.

Wiring for the Kitchen Exhaust System

For updraft exhaust systems, an outlet is often placed in the back of the cupboard above the hood or microwave oven. For a peninsula cooktop, where there is no wall behind the cupboard, the power to the hood is hardwired to the house wiring through the area occupied by the vent duct. The electrical drawing should indicate how this is to be handled for your house.

When the fan is remote from the cooktop, to help reduce the noise, be sure this shows on the drawings so that the wiring is put in place at the right time.

Cabinets

You will need to select a manufacturer for your cabinets, or at least agree with the builder's selection. Most custom home builders use a local custom cabinet shop. You may want to seriously look at using pre-manufactured cabinets if they'll fit into your kitchen. Quality cabinets are available from both custom shops and distributors of pre-manufactured types. Pre-manufactured cabinets are less expensive but the kitchen layout should be designed to accommodate the available cabinet sizes. Read Appendix J before you decide.

Decide how high your cabinets will be. Should they to go all the way to the ceiling or stop at normal height, about seven feet above the floor? If you use an updraft exhaust hood and the exhaust duct is across the top of the cabinets, then tall cabinets are disadvantageous.

Soffits

If the cabinets don't go to the ceiling, decide if the soffits above them are to be boxed in or left open. If you use an updraft exhaust hood, the soffits will have to be boxed in to cover the duct work.

(Sometimes builders find ways to put the ducts in the wall behind the hood but this is not the usual case.) If wallboard corners are rounded in the rest of the house, be sure to specify that those above the cabinets are treated the same way.

Don't have center mullions in your cabinets—they get in the way, are unnecessary, and make it impossible to put pull-out shelves in a cabinet.

The Pantry

Both walk-in and cabinet pantries are seen in today's house plans. There are advantages and disadvantages to each.

Walk-in pantries should be convenient to the kitchen working area. Take a hard look at walk-in pantries to figure out just how useful they will be. Pay particular attention to how much useful shelf space you have. Also, make sure that when you open the pantry door, you're not blocking access to shelves.

Cabinet-type pantries are usually a continuation of the cabinets in the kitchen and have the same depth as the under-counter cabinets, that is, about two feet. If these don't have pull-out shelves, the back half won't be useful unless you enjoy unloading the front part of the shelf to get to something in the back. Perhaps you'd prefer door-like panels with narrow shelves on them inside the cupboard. You can swing these out of the way to get to a third set of shelves in the back of the pantry.

Outlets in Islands and Peninsulas

The National Electrical Code requires that there be at least one outlet in an island or peninsula. Careless, unthinking electricians will sometimes put these where they stick out like a sore thumb in a beautiful hardwood cabinet. Insist on having a say in precisely where this outlet is placed. It's not a bad idea to wait until after the cabinets are installed before you make the decision. Alternatively, consider having the outlet(s) completely hidden by mounting them face downward under the countertop overhang.

The Countertop

Appendix K describes the various kinds of countertops available. Your choices for a kitchen are laminate, ceramic tile, solid-surface, and stone. In the some areas, laminate is the most commonly used countertop, even in upper-level houses. Elsewhere, tile is the standard, with solid-surface materials going into the more expensive homes. Stone is rarely used.

For tile, try to pick a tile pattern which has the front lip pieces which are the same size (length) as the tile itself. Then insist that the installer make the lines of grout for the front pieces and the rest of the counter symmetrical.

If your peninsula or island is to be used in an eating bar, be sure that the countertop is wide enough to provide knee space under it. About 12" is a minimum counter overhang.

If the countertop is tile or solid-surface, you have the opportunity to have a sink which does not have an annoying lip sitting on top of the counter. Tile-in and undercounter sinks, cannot, however, be used with laminate countertops.

A solid-surface counter with the sink lip on top.

A solid-surface counter with a separate undercounter sink.

A tile counter with an under- counter sink.

With tile, a dark colored grout is preferable in terms of maintenance. Light grouts show stains much easier than dark ones. Sealants are available to help this problem but these are tedious to use and have to be re-applied periodically to be effective.

Consider if you want the tiles to be laid parallel with the front of the countertop or on the diagonal. Putting them diagonally gives a little touch of not being quite so ordinary but it does involve more cut tile.

Where tile has to be cut, specify:

1. That there are to be no chipped edges.

2. That the edges be smoothed and rounded.

Regardless of the type of countertop you get, it should include a backsplash and a lip which keeps water and spills from running on the floor. Laminate counters are available with the laminate molded to provide the counter, the backsplash and the bullnose as a single piece. But in some areas like the Pacific Northwest home buyers get their laminate counters made with the backsplash as a separate piece and without the front lip. If you decide on laminates, check out the numerous ways which counter makers use to make them a little more attractive.

Chapter 9

Bed and Bath

Bedrooms and bathrooms require critical decisions about lighting, furniture placement, windows, and outlet locations. As elsewhere, if you don't make the decisions, they'll be made for you.

Bedrooms

Lighting

There are five different arrangements for lights in bedrooms.

- No fixture. The power to an outlet is controlled by the room light switch and the light is provided by a plug-in lamp. This is the least expensive and is the usual California and Arizona set up.

- Room-center fixture. A ceiling fixture, usually small, is located in the center of the room. It is controlled by the room light switch. This is a common arrangement outside of California and Arizona.

- Recessed can lights in front of closets. One or more lights are placed in the ceiling to illuminate the room and particularly the closet. This is also common outside of California and Arizona.

- A ceiling fan is provided with a light kit which is controlled by a wall switch. This is used less commonly.

- Indirect ceiling lighting is sometimes used in large bedrooms with high ceilings to give a dramatic effect.

If the room-center fixture might be changed to a ceiling fan in the future, the mounting box should be strong enough to support the fan and a 3-wire conductor should be used to the wall switch location.

You'll need to decide what you want in each of the bedrooms. The recommendation is to go along with local custom unless you have a reason to use a different option.

The Master Bedroom

Furniture Placement—The master bedroom, like the dining room, is often designed without any thought for placing furniture along the walls. A typical master bedroom suite consists of the bed, two night stands, a large dresser, and a chest or armoire. Besides these, there is often a TV stand or a wall unit for holding the TV, books, etc. When the designer includes lots of windows and unusual wall angles, there is simply no room for the chest or armoire.

Doors—Double entrance doors have the same potential problems in the master bedroom as elsewhere: they can block light switches and take up useful wall space, leaving no room for furniture. In some designs the walk-in closet door swings into the bedroom rather than the closet. This takes away from valuable wall space in the bedroom. A pocket door should be used instead.

Windows—Large windows on the south and west sides of the house can be sun problems in the summer; if possible, face any large windows east or north. Windows, of course, should not go in walls that are needed for furniture.

TV and Phone Outlet—Pick the TV outlet placement carefully. Usually, there is only one wall on which a large dresser can be placed. The TV outlet shouldn't be on this wall unless you want the TV sitting on the dresser. Be sure the telephone jack is around the head of the bed so the telephone itself can sit on one of the night stands.

Bathrooms

Bathrooms with Two Doors

Some halls or guest baths are made with two entry doors. These doors are usually from two bedrooms or from one bedroom and the hall. In some cases, these doors open into a room with a vanity counter and two wash basins, allowing two members of the family to shave, wash, put on makeup, etc., at the same time. From this vanity area, another door leads into a separate room with the toilet and shower and/or tub.

In other arrangements the dual basins, toilet, and shower and/or tub are all in the same room. It's not clear, in this case, what the advantage is in having two basins because one person usually ties up the whole bathroom. Check this arrangement carefully when you run across it to see if it fits your needs.

When checking out bathrooms in floor plans, the obvious things to look for are tubs, showers, and the number and locations of wash basins. But there are other design considerations.

Auxiliary Hot Water

Small hot water heaters are available that mount under a vanity counter to provide hot water immediately. If you want one for a shower or tub, the heater will need to be bigger than one that furnishes water to basins only. As with other hot water heaters, you'll need gas or electricity brought to the heater's location. The feasibility of doing this and the cost will depend on how big a heater you'll need and on the impact it may have on the rest of the house design.

Picture Windows in Bathrooms

The trend in the master bedroom suite is to put the bath tub beside a large picture window. The tub is often in a corner so that there are windows on two sides. (At least one California builder put a large clear glass window on one side of the shower stall!) Windows give a feeling of openness and often provide a great view. The question is, what kind of window treatment is appropriate? Almost any covering you install can only be opened and closed by taking off your shoes and climbing through the tub!

Here are some options:

1. Put permanent coverings over the windows to ensure privacy. Beware, though—you'll lose the openness that was so attractive at first.

2. Install mini-blinds that you adjust by climbing into the tub. If you find the right adjustment that allows you to let in some light while preventing people from seeing in, even at night, then don't readjust the blinds.

3. Get blinds with motorized controls.

4. Use pleated cloth shades that close from the bottom up. Close them up far enough for privacy, but not so far that you block out all natural light. Again, you'll lose your view.

5. The builder of an expensive, single-story home in Eugene, Oregon handled this problem by building a fence a few feet out from the window. Again, no view.

Other ways to let in outside light include replacing windows with glass blocks, stained glass windows, sandblasted window panes, or smaller windows placed high up on the walls. You may want to consider acrylic blocks, which are less expensive than glass blocks for both the material and installation. These are available in clear and several colors.

A way to have light and a feeling of openness while maintaining privacy was seen in a house in Tracy, California. The builder put windows high-up on the wall which were met at the ceiling by skylights above the tub. If this appeals to you, be careful of the potential summer sun problem, particularly if the arrangement faces south or west.

Whirlpool Pump Access

Whirlpool tubs can be expensive, and you probably won't recoup your costs when you sell the house. It's a good idea to talk to a few people who have them and get their reactions. Some people swear by them but many more say they're never used.

If you decide you want a whirlpool tub, don't forget the access door for the pump. This access is seldom needed but it must be there if the pump ever needs attention. There's no reason the access door has to be an eyesore, but it often is.

The options for the location of the access door include:

1. A panel on the side of the tub. If done nicely this can be unobtrusive but it won't work if the side of the tub is covered with tile. It is also not acceptable if the pump is so far behind the access door that it cannot be reached.

2. In a room which backs up to the tub. Closets are the usual location for this option but bedrooms and laundry rooms are also used. But be careful if the door is located in the room with the toilet because it may be so crowded that it becomes necessary to remove the toilet to work on the pump.

3. An outside wall. This is done commonly in California even when it's on the second floor. Good weather-proofing is required for this arrangement.

Towel Rods

Many modern-day bathrooms are open and commodious. There are mirrors, doors, a tub with its surround, and lots of glass but no sensible place to put a towel rod. In the processing of putting all of this luxury into the bath, designers and builders will forget that function should come before form and leave no place for towel rods. Look carefully at the plans for the bathroom to be sure that there is a place for towel rods, hopefully next to the shower and the tub. This shortcoming is more prevalent in California and other places with big airy bathrooms.

Some designs will have no place to put a towel rod next to a wash basin. Watch for this one, too.

Cabinets

Medicine cabinets are not only utilitarian, they can also improve the appearance of a bathroom, but they are simply not used in some regions. If you want one in your house and you are building where they are not common you, may have to use extra care to be sure that your wants get translated into reality.

Medicine cabinets are usually mounted in walls between studs. Be careful that there are instructions for the framers to leave room between studs to mount medicine cabinets. Be sure there is nothing else between the studs, such as pipes or wiring. Don't plan on using an outside wall for the medicine cabinet, because the insulation in the wall will prevent it.

An alternative to a medicine cabinet is to put a cabinet on the wall above the toilet. This option has a couple of disadvantages: 1) the toilet is in the way when you want to get into the cabinet, and 2) if you accidentally drop something or brush it off of a shelf, it's likely to land in the water.

Can You Sidle?

Many master bedroom suites place the toilet in its own small room or in a room with the shower. In model after model, the doors open into the small rooms, forcing you to sidle in beside the toilet bowl to have enough room to close the door. The same arrangement is also seen in many floor plans where the toilet bowl may not be to scale. An alternative is to leave the door off altogether. This is done in some floor plans.

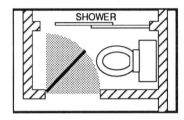

Sidle anyone? The problem
with the door isn't obvious
when it's missing in a model
or a floor plan.

Lighting

Light bars and fluorescent lights are frequently used to illuminate
a vanity area. They cause few shadows when applying make up or
shaving. Some people prefer the skin tones brought out by incandescent lamps in light bars even though fluorescents use less electricity and generate less heat.

Windows and skylights are also used to provide lighting. The need
for concern about excessive summer solar heat through glass was
discussed in Chapter 7. It is a particular problem in small areas like
bathrooms.

Exhaust Fans

Baths and showers should have exhaust fans even if not required
by code. Fans can help reduce the amount of moisture which, in
turn, helps control mildew. Fans, plain lights, and heat lamps should
all have different switches, since not all of them are needed every
time someone uses the room. The kinds of plain lights, lights with
exhaust fans, and heat lamps should all be spelled out in the electrical specifications. And, if it matters to you, be specific about their
exact locations. The electrician will do the best he can but he can't
read your mind.

Tubs

Select a tub by manufacturer and model number, or let the builder
do it for you and hope you end up with something you like in terms
of style, material, and price. Your local plumbing supply store
should be able to explain the pros and cons of the various available
tubs, but not all of them can or will. It is probably prudent to visit
more than one supply store and ask your questions. That way you
stand a better chance of making the right decisions.

In some locations, particularly in California, cultured-marble manufacturers make some really exotic appearing tubs which may

appeal to you. These units are very heavy and the cost of shipping them is exorbitant, but, if they are made locally, you may want to consider them. (If you buy one, be sure it's certified by the national cultured marble organization as explained in Appendix K.)

Your choices for the surrounds are ceramic tile, cultured marble, and marble. Don't consider plastic laminates, they make unattractive surrounds. It's common to use the same material for the tub surround and vanity countertop. Note that the material used for the tub deck may also be used on the front of the tub, making it a true 'surround.'

Showers

While you're at the plumbing supply store, look at shower enclosures. Molded fiberglass units—both those with a gel coat surface and those made with acrylic—are popular. Cultured marble is another option. Since it has no grout, cultured marble does not support mildew growth, and its smooth surface is easy to keep clean. If you live in an area where cultured marble is not commonly seen in new houses, you may be surprised at how handsome it can look.

Ceramic tile is another popular shower enclosure. While mildew is not as serious a problem as it used to be, shower stalls need to be watched in the damper climates. Be sure that tile is mounted on a waterproof board.

All shower stalls should have a hand hold in them. You need something to hold onto while you're standing on one foot washing the bottom of the other one. Don't forget to insist on a slip-proof tile for the bottom of the shower!

Vanity Countertops

The three materials usually used for vanity counters are plastic laminate, tile and cultured marble with regional differences playing a large role in what may be commonly found in your area. Appendix K discusses these differences and the advantages and disadvantages of each material.

With vanity countertops only cultured marble (or the rarely used solid-surface materials) offers the possibility of undercounter mounting of the wash basins. With both plastic laminate and tile counters, the sink is dropped in, that is, it sits on top of the counter with the get-in-the-way lip around it. (Tile counters can be made with an undercounter basin but the appearance is so unattractive that they are seldom used.)

Chapter 10

Other Areas in the Home

We have gone over the kitchen, the bedrooms and the baths. This chapter discusses the other interior areas; the entry, hallways, stairs, dining room, laundry and garage.

The Entry

The entry may be a separate room or it may be a part of a great room encompassing the living room, dining room, and/or family room. Stairs, if there are any, usually start from the entry. Although a large entry can add to the feeling of luxury in a house, it is an area that is not used that much. You may want to make it fairly small, saving the floor space for something more useful.

Floors

Even without separate walls, the entry is usually an identifiable area. This is accomplished using a different floor covering than adjacent rooms or, as is commonly done in the southwestern architecture of southern California, by making the entry raised, requiring a step down to the rest of the house. Floor coverings need to stand up to water and mud, so carpet is rarely used. The most common entry materials include linoleum, ceramic tile, marble, stone, and hardwoods. For safety reasons, be sure the material used isn't slippery when wet.

Fixtures

In many floor plans the entry way is not centered on the front door, particularly if the entry is a part of a great room. When this is the case the entry fixture(s) may be centered on the door itself or may be centered over the entry way. If you don't tell the electrician what you want, you'll get what he likes.

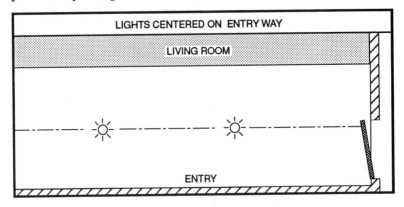

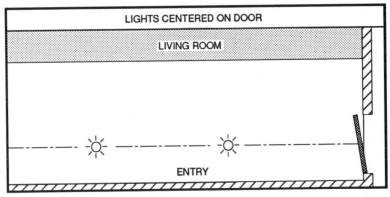

Lights may be centered on either the entry way or on the front door. It's your decision.

Hallways and Stairways

These two areas are among those we call non-living space. They are called "ways" for good reason. They neither hold furniture nor are they areas where we spend any time. In more extravagant house designs they can be eye-catchers or even dramatic; like a wide curving staircase, or a bridge between two upstairs living areas.

Stairway Design

Luxurious stairs are easy to climb but take a lot of floor space while steep stairs take less space but are difficult to use. Some designers tend to make stairs too steep for comfortable use and you need to let them know what you want.

A good angle for the stairs is about 36 degrees with a riser height of 7¼". Each step width should be close to 11½" including 1½" of nosing. (The riser is the vertical board between steps and the nosing is the part of the tread that sticks out over it.)

Building codes usually require a minimum stair width of 36". You may want more. Similarly, codes require a minimum head room of 6' 8". Again you should consider more, say 7' 0", to give a more open feeling.

Stairway Lighting

Have you seen chandeliers that require scaffolding to change a light bulb? *Caveat Emptor!* Consider some of the alternatives. One is to put sconces along the staircase and/or on the landing to light the stairs. Another scheme is to used several unobtrusive night-light type fixtures which are mounted a couple of feet above the treads in the stair well. These units may be small (the size of a standard outlet cover plate) or they may be two or three times larger. They're installed flush with the staircase wall and have louvers in them to direct the light downward.

Lighting in Hallways

Most of the time, light fixtures are placed in the center of the hall where there's nothing in particular that needs lighting. Hall lights should be in front of closets where they're needed. For the same reason have a light installed in the hall at the thermostat location.

The Dining Room

In small starter houses the dining room is often omitted. The idea is that a young family has better uses for the space than for a room that seldom gets used and requires a significant outlay for furniture. If you decide to do without a dining room, be sure the kitchen eating area is large enough to accommodate your family and guests.

Today's formal dining room isn't always a separate room. Often, it's an area in a great room set aside for the dining room furniture. Ways to distinguish it include using archways, partial walls, and columns, or changing the ceiling height or pitch, flow of a wall, or the pattern in a heavily textured ceiling.

Designers and builders hesitate to commit any more space to the formal dining room than they can get away with. Home buyers recognize that dining rooms aren't used all that often, so they're torn between saving money and making the room big enough to accommodate a full-size set of dining room furniture. Unfortunately, the answer to this problem in many of today's designs is to include a formal dining room in the floor plan and then make it so small that it won't take a set of furniture.

Room Dimensions and Furniture Placement

- When we moved into our house in southern California, we had a separate formal dining room that barely held our dining room furniture. When we decided to replace our old furniture with a nicer set, there was no longer enough room. Whenever we entertained it was difficult to pull out the chairs so people could sit down and almost impossible to get behind chairs with people sitting in them.

  At least we could extend the table on out into the family room to seat everyone when we hosted the family Thanksgiving dinner.

  Our present dining room doesn't use much more floor space but it's open on two sides. What a difference. We have room behind the chairs and enough space to expand the table for large gatherings.

When deciding on the size of the dining room, don't forget that, even if your present dinette set will fit, you should leave yourself room to get a full sized dining set in the future. And don't forget that when you sell, your would-be buyers will be interested in a home which will house their full-sized dining room furniture.

Wall space in a dining room is a precious commodity. There must be room for a hutch or china cabinet. Some dining room sets include a server and there must also be room for that along a wall.

The table is usually put in the center of the room and the dining room arrangement should be able to accommodate extending the table for large parties. This is often into an adjacent room or area.

A dining room table is typically about 42" × 72". With people seated in chairs at the table another 36" on each side of the table is needed so that people can get behind the chairs.

A typical china cabinet is 22" to 24" deep so that the minimum dining room width is 136" or 11' 4". The commonly-used 10' wide dining room just isn't enough.

The length of the room without additional leaves in the table and with someone seated at each end of the table is 144" or 12'. If there is no way to extend the table into an adjacent room or area then the dining room needs to be 32" longer.

Any doors which extend into the area occupied by the table and chairs also need to be considered.

This is a lot of room for a small house. Clever combining of the dining room with an adjacent room can cut this down significantly without compromising the amount of room needed for the table and chairs. With dining rooms which have three or four walls, it is not possible to take advantage of the presence of the adjacent rooms.

Watch out for sunken living rooms. A dining room table cannot be extended in that direction. Unfortunately, it is easier to remember this after you've already moved into your new home.

The Chandelier

One of the more disturbing things seen in many of today's houses is the inattention paid to how the furniture will look in the dining room. In particular, the chandelier should be centered over the table. To do otherwise is visually jarring. Unfortunately that is something which many times cannot be fixed after you move in. Planning ahead is critical if you do not want to live with this user-unfriendly irritation.

Some contemporary home designs have forgone the traditional dining room chandelier in favor of recessed ceiling lights. They obviously do not have the potential problems with chandelier location discussed here.

The Chandelier and Furniture—As discussed above, in many cases the table is offset between the sides of the dining room to allow for a china hutch on one wall. To have the chandelier centered above the table it must also be offset relative to the sides of the room.

If the electrician has not been thinking ahead or you don't make a point of it, you'll end up swagging the chandelier as shown in the illustration. Swagged fixtures are almost always the result of not thinking ahead. Don't let it happen to you.

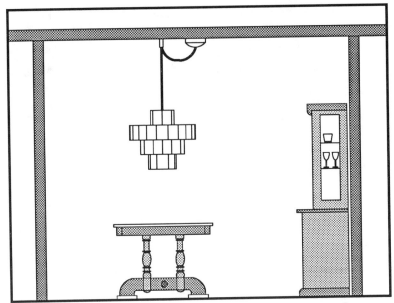

A swagged chandelier is needed when the electrician installs the mounting box in the center of the room.

Ceiling Treatment—Be wary of special ceiling treatments such as coved, trayed, coffered, Pullman, Gambrel or any other arrangement which results in a ceiling pattern that is symmetrical around the center of the room. These all dictate that the chandelier be centered in the pattern, i.e., at the room center. If the room isn't large enough to allow the table to also be centered, you'll have the problem discussed above only this time you can't swag the chandelier to fix it.

High Ceilings—Many homes in the southwest have a similar problem arising from the high ceilings used to get the open airy feeling in the architectural design. In this case the chain holding the chandelier is quite long and, visually, it becomes an important part of the dining room. Because it is so obvious, it should be symmetrical with regard to the tall room walls. Putting it off center simply doesn't look right.

And again, there is a chandelier which is centered between the walls which should only be used with a dining room table which is also centered.

Minimum Room Size—If you use a special pattern or if you have high parallel walls in your dining room, you should be sure your room is big enough to let you put a china hutch along one wall and still center the table. The room sizes required for this are:

- If the hutch is parallel with the table: 14' wide by 15' long.
- If the hutch is at the end of the table: 12' wide by 17' long.

Windows in Dining Rooms

Many floor plans have a window in the dining room. Be careful of this window if it is close to being centered on the dining room table.

- In a furnished model home in Agoura, California the floor plan is laid out so that the dining room table is parallel to the wall with the hutch. The chandelier was hung in the center of the room and a window was centered there too. The end of the table was close to the window. However, for the reasons discussed earlier, the table could not be placed in the center of room so that it was about a foot off from the chandelier and also about a foot off from the center of the window. The disymmetry of the table and the window was probably more jarring than the table and the chandelier.

In any case, be careful of arrangements like these. If there is a window in the dining room, take care that it is not located where it looks like it was meant to be centered on the table but never quite made it. Unless the window would look out on a view, you might consider omitting the window and using skylights for the dining room instead.

The Family Room

If you are going to have a gas fireplace, then the location of the fireplace becomes important so that you can use a direct vent unit as discussed in Appendix E. Besides that, you need to be careful where the fireplace is relative to the TV. The fireplace and the TV should be close to each other so that same furniture arrangement is used to enjoy both. But you don't want the TV where a window can cause a glare on the screen during the day.

The location of the TV outlet needs to be addressed while keeping the foregoing thoughts in mind.

Ceiling fans are common in family rooms, and the earlier admonitions about running 3-wire power conductors apply here also.

The Utility Tub

Many builders and designers do not include a laundry or utility tub in their houses. Most home users want one. You should consider whether you want yours in the laundry room or in the garage.

For pre-soaking especially dirty clothes, the tub is more convenient in the laundry. For cleaning tools, for cleanup after yard work and after play, the tub is better off in the garage. In the garage the faucet on the tub can also be used as a hose connection.

If your house plans permit a special heated 'mud' room for the utility tub, that's even better.

The Laundry Room

You will have to decide early whether to plan for a gas or an electric dryer. This is often a regional consideration; gas is the norm in southern California while electricity is used in northern California and the Pacific Northwest. Even when you start with electricity, having the laundry plumbed for gas will make it possible to change over to the less expensive energy in the future. It will also make the house more attractive to buyers when the time comes.

The laundry can be a simple niche off of a hallway, it can be a separate room including ironing board and a broom closet, or it can be missing entirely with washer and dryer in the garage. Whichever arrangement you choose here are some things which should be kept in mind:

- Washers and dryers are noisy. Choose the location carefully. Consider noise insulation. Don't use louvered doors.

- Dryer doors open downward or they are hinged on the right side. Therefore put the dryer on the right of the washer so the door isn't in the way when moving clothes between them.

  Put the washer and dryer right next to each other. Separating them will mean extra steps and dripping laundry.

  If you have a tub in the laundry room, put it on the left of the washer. If you have a clothes folding area, put it on the right side of the dryer.

- Be sure there is a light over the washer which illuminates the interior of the washing machine even when you are leaning over it. This is a common shortcoming, one you'll appreciate when you try to find a sock inside an unlit washer.

• Don't let the builder run the duct from the dryer to the front of the house where lint can become an eyesore. Be sure there's a rodent-proof flap over the end of the duct.

• Be sure that the connection for the dryer duct inside the laundry is where it can be useful. Sloppy workmanship sometimes leaves the duct where it is almost impossible to connect to it.

The Garage

Garage Design

Finishing (wallboard and painting) the inside of the garage is something for which there is no standard practice. For energy code and fire code reasons, common walls between the house and the garage will always be insulated and wallboard installed. Beyond that, you should specify just what you want done: what's to be insulated and to what R-value and what's to be covered with wallboard and how it's to be finished.

Garage doors (the big ones you drive your car through) may be metal or wood. The metal ones require less maintenance and last longer but are more expensive. Wooden doors that are only a year or two old but face the direction of the sun and of winter storms usually are in need of a coat of paint.

Whether and how many garage door openers are to be furnished by the builder is an item that you should specify, otherwise you may not get any because for this, too, there is no standard.

Unless the garage is just stuck onto the end of the house, the size of the garage in a given design is pretty well fixed. You should check if it's adequate for you. A difference of two feet in width and/or length can easily make the difference between being crowded and having room to put in a work bench and storage cupboards. As a starting point consider that less than 22' × 22' will be a crowded double garage.

If you want, your builder probably can change one double garage door to two singles or vice versa.

Garage Wiring

Check the electrical schematic for outlets in the garage. Some houses are designed to have only the one that is required by the National Electrical Code. You will want at least one on each wall of the garage. These can all be on the same 15-ampere circuit and must be GFCI protected. If you have a freezer or other appliance in the garage you should put it on a separate circuit and not reduce the available capacity in the other outlets. It is a good idea to GFCI protect this outlet, too, even if it is not absolutely required by code. It is appropriate to specify exactly what you want and not leave it to the electrician and building inspector to do things right.

The designer's drawings should show power going to outlets for the garage door opener(s). It is convenient to have a switch in this line to shut off the openers when you are on vacation. The options for doing this are given in Appendix M.

Garage Lighting

In some places it is customary to put one light socket in the garage for each car that may be parked there. In others, one socket is supposed to serve the whole garage. If your plan shows only one, then increase the number of sockets so that there is a modicum of light even in the dark of night. You may want more than one per car stall or you may want the electrician to install fluorescent shop lights for you or at least put in suitable sockets so you can install them yourself.

If you ever came in the side garage door of your house at night and stumbled around to get to the light switch at the door into the house then you'll appreciate the suggestion that you have the garage lights wired with two switches in a 3-way operation, putting the second switch at the sidedoor.

Garage Sidedoor

Some designs show a garage sidedoor and others do not. Unless the garage is dug back into a hillside you should be able to have a sidedoor if you want. The door may be metal or wood but, as with the big doors, metal will last longer and appearance is not critical. The door hinges and the dead bolt striker plate should be mounted with long screws for security reasons as discussed in Appendix M.

A sidedoor with a window in it is a further security consideration. If you are thinking of such a window, the appendix is worth checking.

Garage Floor

With areas of concrete as large as a garage floor there will be cracking when the floor settles. To control where this cracking occurs, the concrete subcontractor puts dividers in the floor before the concrete is poured. These dividers (about ½" by 4") are set on edge just below the surface of the concrete. If a trowelled line is made in the floor above each divider the inevitable cracking will occur at the bottom of the line. If this line is not put in the concrete, the cracking will be in a jagged unattractive line the length of the garage. Besides its appearance, this is hard to keep clean. Be sure to include a requirement for the dividing trowelled line.

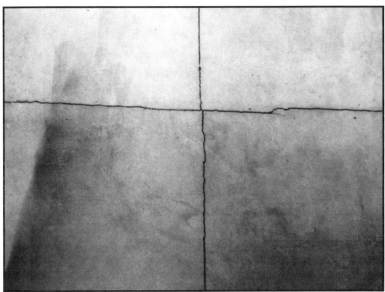

The crack in the garage floor need not look like this.

"We shape our buildings, thereafter they shape us."

Winston Churchill

Chapter 11

Outside the House

A first step in considering what materials to use on your house is to check the CC&Rs. Many of them will spell out what is possible and what is not. Even if they're decades old and out of date, they're still the law of the land where your lot is concerned.

• A builder bought a lot in an older Pacific Northwest neighborhood where the CC&Rs said that the roofs were to be cedar shake. At least one house had already been built in the subdivision using Woodruf (discussed below) which is frequently an acceptable alternative to shake. However, when the fellow across the street heard that Woodruf was planned for the new house he let it be known loud and clear that he'd go to court if the roof were not cedar shake.

Not wanting to have the property tied up in time consuming litigation, the builder caved in and built the house with cedar shake. If you don't want to get caught in a similar fix, read your CC&Rs before you buy the lot and then check what they say again before you start construction.

Exterior Materials

The exterior material you choose for your house will depend on your personal taste, cost, the general availability in your area, its suitability for your climate, its consistency with the house's architecture, and its congruity with the neighborhood where you plan to build.

Stucco is used almost exclusively in Arizona and southern California, with occasional wood, brick, or stone accents. In northern California, house exteriors can be just about anything. Stucco is popular because of its practicality and low cost.

You'll find that the use of actual wood is infrequent. Builders prefer a composite board or hardboard that's made to look like wooden boards, shake, or siding. This material virtually eliminates the problems of warping and splitting that can raise havoc with boards and shake. In general, it is also less expensive.

Stone and brick are not used in many areas as the primary exterior material because of the cost to reinforce it against earthquakes.

In damper climates, some stucco is used but almost all house exteriors are wood or wood products. Stucco may develop cracks with time and it could let water into the wall space that will never dry out. To overcome this problem, stucco-like synthetic materials are now used. These are more expensive than lap siding but less expensive than masonry (brick or stone).

A problem with stucco is that it stains easily. This was seen in a tract in Riverside, California which the mortgage company got from the builder after foreclosure. These two-story houses had no rain gutters, very small eaves, and little landscaping. Water running off of the roofs splashed mud up onto the stucco and permanently stained it. It's important, particularly with stucco, to get gutters on the houses as soon as possible to prevent this from happening.

Stucco stains when mud splashes on it. This house had no gutters.

In northern California a common material used on exteriors is a hardboard siding with a wood-textured finish that's relatively inexpensive and easy to install. This material was also seen on the fronts of some southern California houses. It's not stocked in the northwest and is available there only on special order.

If you are making every effort to keep costs down, consider using one material on the front of the house for appearance and a less expensive material for the sides and back. In northern California many houses use the board-like hardboard material on the street side and stucco elsewhere. In the Pacific Northwest the idea is embodied in houses with lap siding on the front and T1-11 on the sides and back. (T1-11 is a composite wood material made to have the appearance of vertical boards.)

Another option that's getting more attention every time the cost of lumber increases is the use of vinyl siding. This material has an indefinite lifetime and never needs painting. It's more easily damaged by physical abuse than are the sturdier materials.

Your builder or local building supply house will be able to tell you the options available in your area and their relative costs.

Roofs

Rain Gutters

It's a good idea to have gutters included with the house when it's built, regardless of where you live.

In parts of southern California and Arizona, builders rarely include rain gutters as a part of the houses they build. In the Pacific Northwest no one even thinks about them because they're always included with the house you buy. A set of gutters can run well over $1000, so don't dismiss them as trivial when you buy in areas where they're not ordinarily included.

Gutters may be plastic, aluminum, or heavily galvanized and painted steel. Gutters are available in two sizes; a larger one that completely covers a 6" fascia and a smaller one that covers part of the fascia. The choice is primarily one of cost vs. appearance.

All northwest builders and some California builders include drain lines from the down spouts to the street. Others just dump the water into the yard. Unless the soil is particularly porous, you may have a problem if the drains are missing. It's not a big thing to have the drain lines included if you have a downhill shot to the street. Having them is one less thing to worry about after you move in.

Roofing Materials

There are six commonly used roofing materials:

• Concrete tile or shake
• Clay tile
• Cedar shake
• Woodruf, a hard-board material that simulates shake
• Architectural composition roofing
• Asphalt shingles

Concrete Tile—Concrete tile or concrete shake comes in many shapes and colors. It has the longest life of any of the materials. It's not damaged by weather or age but it will break when walked on. (It can also be broken by golf balls if you live on a golf course.) It is, obviously, fireproof. It is the most expensive roof, not only because of the cost of the material itself but, being concrete, it's heavy and may need a sturdier roof structure to support it. Its weight and the ease with which the pieces can be broken make it more difficult to install, all adding to the cost of the roof.

Clay Tile—Clay tile is a low-fired brick-like material. It is usually made in the form of a half of a red tile pipe. It has been used for several hundred years in southwestern architecture but has given way to its concrete counterpart because of the greater sturdiness. Clay is even more subject to damage from being walked on or hit with golf balls but is less expensive than concrete.

You'll usually get back some of the initial extra cost of these non-flammable materials through lower insurance rates. This is something you'll need to check. In general, the 'carrots' for using concrete tiles or concrete shakes are fire resistance and near-zero maintenance costs.

Cedar Shake—Split cedar shake has been a popular roofing material for a long time. It's perceived as being the luxury material in many areas. Unfortunately, the quality of available shake has declined. Today, it's the shortest-lived modern-day roofing material except for the cheapest asphalt shingles. It requires more maintenance than any of the others. It's very flammable ("tinder box" is a term that is often used) which results in higher fire insurance premiums. It's more expensive than other materials except concrete tile. Yet, in the Pacific Northwest, it's still very popular. CC&Rs in many exclusive developments allow only cedar shake, concrete tile, or concrete shake roofs for appearance reasons. In these developments, cedar shake is seen much more often than concrete tile. Obviously, personal taste figures heavily in this matter. This is unfortunate because cedar shake is, by far, the worst buy in roofing materials available today.

Woodruf—A material with the trademark "Woodruf" is manufactured by the Masonite Corporation as an alternative to shake. It's a composite wood product with an appearance similar to shake, but more uniform. It's less expensive than shake and is often permitted where CC&Rs spell out shake or tile. The expected life of a roof of this material (15 years) is about the same as a cedar shake roof but not longer than concrete tile or the better grades of composition roofing. It, too, will burn but not with the same vigor as cedar shake.

Composition Roofing—Architectural composition roofing is an improved, fiberglass-reinforced version of the old asphalt roofing which has been around for many years. It's a flat material that's installed very quickly using a staple gun. It comes in a number of colors to match the house. It's less expensive than most other roofing materials and comes in a wide range of guarantees and prices. It doesn't burn as readily as shake. Walking on it does not harm it as much as other materials.

Asphalt Shingles—Asphalt shingles are the least expensive material and are short-lived. They're seldom used even on the least expensive new homes.

Your builder can go over the costs of the various materials with you. Whether you go with concrete tile for its durability, shake for its appearance, or composition roofing for its cost is a personal choice. But don't forget perceptions, because they can be very important when you try to sell your house.

- In a tract near Sacramento, California, it was noted that the first phase had cedar shake roofs, the second had architectural composition, and the newest phase used concrete shake. The builder explained that after the Oakland fire storm, nobody wanted anything to do with cedar shake and that architectural comp is simply not accepted, because it's viewed as a cheap material used mostly for replacing older asphalt roofs.

- Unlike the Pacific Northwest, the only place where architectural comp was seen on new houses in California were on the lowest-priced starter homes. Regional perceptions can be strong indeed.

In some areas, the under side of roof eave overhangs (soffits) are commonly left open and in others they're closed in. When vinyl siding is used, vinyl pieces are designed to close in the soffits. With other siding, soffits are closed in with plywood which is fitted under the overhanging roof beams. This improves the appearance since it gives a much smoother finish to someone looking up at the underside of the eaves. Closing in is much appreciated when you get around to repainting your house. Whether you want closed-in soffits is a matter of local custom, cost, and your personal preference.

Roof Slope

The slope of the roof is measured in 'pitch' using an expression such as 4/12 which means there is a 4" vertical rise for each 12" of roof measured along the horizontal.

In today's houses there is less variation in the slope of roofs than in the past. There are two reasons for this: some roofing materials aren't guaranteed if the roof isn't steep enough and very steep roofs are not popular with builders because of safety concerns for roofers. These concerns translate to higher costs for building steep roofs because of the techniques needed to prevent the installers from falling and because of higher workman's insurance costs.

Overhang

Roof overhangs protect at least part of the house from the direct rays of the summer sun, helping to keep it cooler and provide some protection from rains. In snow climates, roof overhangs serve another important function: they help keep melting snow water from seeping into the house.

During cold weather, snow on a roof can be melted by the heat of the house under it. The water runs under the snow toward the eaves and gutter. An ice dam can form at the roof edge backing up the water and causing the roof to leak. If there is inadequate overhang this water goes into the house.

Roof overhangs are sometimes omitted for reasons of appearance in a particular design and are sometimes made inadequately small for cost-saving reasons. If your house is in an area where it snows, make sure there's a substantial roof overhang, particularly with roofs with lower pitches. (24" is suggested as a nominal value.) In desert areas, much larger overhangs are useful because of the shade they provide against the summer sun.

Protect the Entry

A properly designed house will have a porch with a roof over it in front of the main door. Two advantages of having the porch are that it provides a place for guests to stand when they ring the door bell and it keeps the sun and rain from quickly deteriorating the door itself. This was seen dramatically in one tract in Riverside where, after only one winter, the finish on the doors had broken down and the wood underneath was starting to come apart, particularly on the bottom third where the doors were exposed to both sun and rain. Metal front doors solve the problem, too.

An unprotected house entry.

Nooks and Crannies

Where roofs from dormers meet the rest of the roof there's usually a small protected area that's attractive to birds looking for a place to set up housekeeping. If this is okay by you, fine. If you'd rather the birds took their dirty nests, noisy nestlings, and multitudinous parasitic pests to some tree or bird house, then these protected nooks and crannies in the roof should be blocked off, either with wire mesh or boards.

This can be done at any time. However, it's a good idea for the builder's crew to do this so that you don't have to shoo the birds away when they've already decided to set up housekeeping. In some areas it's illegal to do anything once nesting activities have begun. This is yet another small detail you can put in your specifications or wait and take care of it after you've moved in.

Concrete Work

Sidewalks

Front sidewalks can be utilitarian and ugly, or smooth and flowing with lots of curb appeal. If you don't put your desires in your specifications, you're apt to have a walk that doesn't do a thing for the appearance of the house.

- Don't forget the earlier admonition about not getting a house with a steeply pitched sidewalk if you live where there's ever snow and ice.

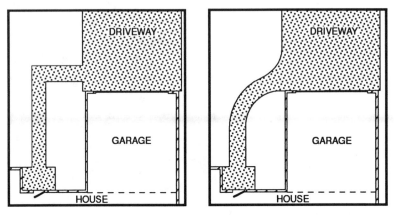

Different front walks (Some builders are right-angle folks)

Steps are better than a steep walk. But be careful with steps. If there's a possibility of someone not seeing the step, better have it marked with white paint to avoid accidents. If you are concerned with access by people with disabilities, you'll want a gently sloping walk without steps.

RV Pads

An RV pad is another item that needs to be considered. Some sub-divisions do not allow them. In others, local custom may frown on the idea of storing an RV on a residential lot. If, however, you want and can have an RV pad, you'll have to be sure that the lot is wide enough for both it and the house. Beyond that, when the builder is working up the cost for the house, be sure there's enough money for concrete to pour a useful driveway for the RV pad. Some driveways/RV pads are too narrow and simply cannot be used by RVs.

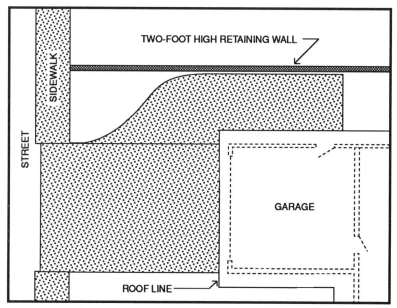

An RV pad that isn't. With the roof overhang, even the smallest RV couldn't get in there.

Conduits Under Concrete

When sidewalks, driveways, and RV pads are being poured be sure you have enough conduits put under them. An eventual irrigation system may need to have a pipe go under a piece of concrete. It's a lot simpler (and cheaper) to put an oversize pipe (conduit) under the walk or driveway before it's poured. You can then put your irrigation pipe(s) through the conduit whenever you need to. Alternately, the concrete subcontractor can lay a piece of ¾" PVC under the concrete for your irrigation system. This is simpler but lacks flexibility.

A more common problem arises with telephone and television cables that are run from the street to your house. When these have to go under concrete, the easiest and most common thing to do is to dig them directly in the dirt before the concrete is poured. If this is done, you'd better pray that nothing ever goes wrong with either of them. The methods of repair are not only expensive but unsightly, unless you don't mind the sight of wires running up the outside of your house.

Have pieces of plastic conduit put under the concrete and then run the telephone and TV cables in the conduit. If a cable ever needs replacing, it's just a matter of pulling a new one through the conduit. Have an extra wire put in the conduit so that it can be used to pull in a new cable if it's ever needed.

- Where needed, be sure that the specifications say the end of the conduits are to come up through the concrete. In one house, the builder instructed the subcontractor to put the telephone and TV cables in conduit under the RV pad. This was done but the end of the conduit wasn't brought up to the surface of the RV pad. Now that the pad is poured, the two cables come up through the concrete just as if there were no conduit underneath.

Electrical power is run in conduits in the first place so those wires should pose no problem.

Decks and Patios

If you're planning a patio, make it as large as you want initially. Don't put in a small one with the intention of expanding it later because, when adding concrete to make it bigger, it is virtually impossible to make it look like it had been poured all in one piece. It will always look like an afterthought.

Decks have similar problems. It's difficult to add on and keep anything like an aesthetically appealing appearance. So unless it's laid out for possible later expansion, make it big enough in the first place.

In considering whether to have a deck or patio, remember that patios are much less expensive than decks by a ratio of about 1:6 and that decks will become even more expensive as the price of lumber increases.

Don't forget to have gas stubbed to the deck or patio area for your BBQ. Even if you don't have a gas BBQ, the guy that's looking at the house when you're ready to sell may find it a very positive feature. Make sure the deck isn't built over the gas stub as I've seen done a couple of times.

Watch the location of the gas stub as well as the electrical outlet on the back of your house. The gas stub is definitely for the BBQ and one of the electrical outlet's uses will be to power the BBQ spit motor. Obviously they should be close to each other and close to where the BBQ is likely to be placed. It seems obvious, but more than one house was seen in which the two were are least 20 feet apart.

If you are having a deck built, have the decking put down with deck screws rather than nails. Screws allow you to remove a board and put it back down. When nails are used, you buy new lumber and try to get a finish on it like the rest of the deck. Screws are also less likely to pull up when boards start to warp.

Electrical

Outside Outlets

In 1993 the National Electrical Code changed the number of required outside outlets from one to two. When this change becomes effective in your area, you won't have to run an extension cord to the back of the house to get power for your Christmas lights or electric lawn mower.

If you have an RV pad, you'll want at least one out there. If you plan to have an outside barbecue with a spit or use an environmentally desirable electric barbecue starter, be sure the outlet in the back of the house is close to where the barbecue will most likely be located.

These outside outlets must be GFCI protected. It's probably a good idea for them to have their own 15A or 20A circuit.

If you're planning for a spa in the backyard, you'll need a separate circuit for it. According to one interpretation of the code, the outlet for the spa doesn't have to be GFCI protected. However, it's a good idea to do it. Anytime you're going to be near a ground or a water pipe and power at the same time, you can't be too careful.

House Numbers

You'll need lights on the front of your house to help guests find you and to see their way to the front door. These lights may be chosen for their aesthetic appearance as well as their functional use of illumination. The lights should also light your house numbers so people can find the house at night.

These lights may be either decorative lights or recessed can lights. Decorative lights are usually mounted on the front of the garage on one or both sides of the door. Another decorative light is then located near the front door. Can lights, as needed to give adequate illumination, are mounted in boxed-in eave soffits.

At the urging of fire and police departments, new homes in some communities use black numbers mounted on white back-lighted plastic. These units, about 5" × 10", are equipped with light sensors which turn them on at night

These unattractive all-houses-alike plastic numbers are not among our suggested solutions for lighting house numbers. It's a simple matter to select fixtures which shed light on the house and then to put the numbers in the light. Be sure to have this done. In over 40% of the houses surveyed the house numbers were not lighted.

 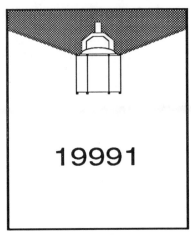

Many lights do not illuminate the house numbers

Lights and Lap Siding

With lap siding, each successive board overlaps the one below it. This is the most popular exterior used on the fronts of houses in the Pacific Northwest. However, when decorative outside lights are mounted on it, there is a problem. The siding slopes, therefore the fixtures slope.

Better builders will fashion a small vertical surface on which to mount the lights and then install the siding around it. Insist on this, if you are planning lap siding.

Under the House

Crawl Space

Be sure there's enough room under the house for a crawl space, not a slither space. The floor beams sit even with the top of the foundation wall but heating ducts and sewer pipes go under the beams, thus cutting into the available space. Heating ducts can be large, and are wrapped with insulation, making them even larger. Make sure you have a minimum of three feet from the dirt to the top of the foundation wall so you can get around easily.

Drainage

Codes don't require drain lines around a house. To handle a potential water problem, the builder grades the dirt under the house to a low spot and installs either a drain or a sump pump.

The dirt under the house is then covered with a heavy plastic polyethylene sheet (Visqueen). Vents around the foundation make it so that the space above the plastic is kept dry, even though the ground underneath may be wet. This keeps the wood under the house from getting dry rot, a fungus that rots wood when it's in a moist environment.

In most places, water doesn't collect under a house and builders and code inspectors get pretty sloppy about what they do and what they allow. When a house is built on a lot with a ground water problem, this sloppiness can turn into a real problem.

Consider this example:

- Construction on a new house was started when the soil was still saturated from the winter rains. The dirt inside the foundation was sloped, more or less, toward one corner of the house. In actuality, the dirt was really just mud that was pushed around with a bulldozer to get something resembling a slope.

At the low corner a drain pipe was put just under the footing. The soil under the house had been graded to be below the bottom of the footing so that the drain pipe sat several inches above the dirt it was supposed to be draining. The plastic sheet was laid down over the mud and water and the house was built.

In an area with no ground-water problem, the water and ground would eventually dry out because of the circulation allowed by vents around the foundation. In this house, however, there was a ground-water problem. The water seeped through the foundation wall, oozed up from below, and collected at the low corner of the crawl space under the house, below the level of the drain. The plastic sheet sank to the bottom of the water and the crawl space turned into a lake.

The problem should never have occurred. The drain pipe, according to the code, should have been at the lowest spot under the house. It wasn't.

Where's the Sump Pump?

To solve a problem with water under the house, sump pumps are sometimes needed to keep the water from collecting. But in one house that I saw, the pump was installed right under the master bedroom. Now in the rainy season the home users have to turn the sump pump off so they can sleep at night and then turn it on the next morning—and hope that the crawl space keeps dry enough to prevent dry rot.

The builder wasn't thinking of the home user when the work for the drainage under the house was being done. Vigilance is necessary. If a sump pump is needed, be sure it's located away from the bedroom area of the house.

Hose Bibbs

You'll want hose bibbs on the outside of your house. Most builders put in two: one in front and one in back. For most of us this isn't enough. If you have an RV pad, you'll want a hose bibb there. In any case, an additional hose bibb on at least one side of the house is useful.

If you need hot water to wash your car, install a bibb, connected to both hot and cold, in the garage. (This works well with the utility tub in the garage as discussed in Chapter 10.)

Specify, either in writing or on a drawing, where you want the hose bibbs. Allow the plumber some freedom in order to minimize the cost of putting them in place, but be sure your wants are known.

In areas where there is danger of water freezing in hose bibbs, plumbing codes require a means of draining the water from the bibbs in the winter. Two methods are permitted; a frost-proof hose bibb or a regular hose bibb with a stop-and-waste valve.

Frost-Proof Hose Bibbs

The frost-proof bibb includes a piece of copper pipe as a part of the bibb itself. This pipe extends the valve part of the bibb back into a part of the house which is heated and where there is no danger of

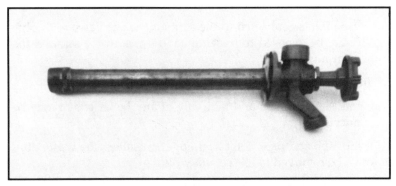

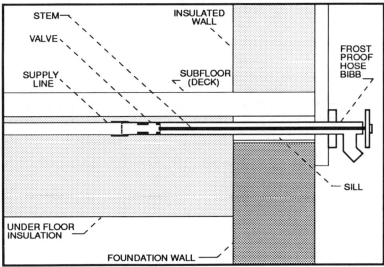

A frost-proof hose bibb.

freezing. When it is turned off, water drains from the exposed part of the hose bibb and no damage occurs.

There is a precaution, however. Sometimes hoses with closed nozzles are left connected to the bibb so that the water cannot drain. This has happened often enough that plumbers in some localities have an aversion to using the bibbs at all. Properly used, they effectively eliminate problems with freezing.

Stop-and-Waste Valves

Stop-and-waste valves are installed in an accessible heated location where there is no danger of freezing. The "stop" part is simply a turn-off valve. The "waste" part is a plug on the valve which can be removed to allow water to drain.

The hose bibb is connected to the stop-and-waste valve with pipe which may be exposed to freezing conditions. In the autumn the home user must:

1. Turn off the water at the stop-and-waste valve.

2. Open the hose bibb and take care of any hoses which may be connected.

3. If the bibb and pipe don't drain by themselves, the waste plug must be removed to let the water out.

Of course, in the spring the above process must be reversed.

Unfortunately, not all plumbers follow the code carefully and not all inspectors see that they do. In far too many cases the stop-and-waste valve is placed where it is not readily accessible, making it virtually useless. If your builder or plumber insists that frost-proof hose bibbs are not a good idea, then you should insist that he put the stop-and-waste valves where you can get to them easily and that pipes drain by simply opening the hose bibb.

Part IV

Fulfillment

Chapter 12

Finding the Right Builder

Finding the right builder is the single most important thing you can do to get the house you want on time and within budget. Two critical characteristics to look for in a builder are integrity and competency.

Integrity

Is the builder honest, reliable, and trustworthy? How do you find out?

When it comes to checking on a builder's reputation, find someone who's competent to judge. Get a list of recently completed homes from the builder and talk to as many of the owners as you can. Ask those owners if they know of any others who have bought houses from the builder. Check to see if these are on the list the builder gave you. Be suspicious if they aren't—the builder may be hiding something.

When talking to the owners try to get a sense of the builder's integrity by asking these questions:

1. Did the builder make a serious attempt to fix things or to recompense the buyer for an error?

2. Were things fixed when promised?

3. Did the builder keep promises about little things as well as the big ones?

4. Was the house finished when it was promised and, if not, how late was it?

Check county recorders' offices for the names of buyers and sellers of all properties in the county. In some counties you can get the names and addresses of all buyers who have bought property from a given seller for as far back as you want. There may be a small fee to generate the data, but it's one way to find the names of buyers the builder didn't tell you about. Another way to get buyers' names, or at least the house addresses, is through the multiple listing service, if the builder had his houses listed there. You have to do this through a real estate broker's office.

Talk to building inspectors to see which builders have the least trouble meeting building code requirements. It's a way to weed out those who try to just get by with the least possible effort.

Check with the local Better Business Bureau. If the builder doesn't belong to the Better Business Bureau, find out why.

Check with the state contractors' board. They'll tell you if there have been any complaints made about the builder. If there are unsatisfied complaints, take your business elsewhere.

You'll probably talk to the builder several times a week while the house is under construction. What kind of rapport do the two of you have? Remember, even with the most detailed contract and specifications, there are always decisions to be made during construction. The builder should keep a detailed checklist of how things have been decided. You should keep one, too. Be nosy. If you see something that you don't understand, ask questions. If, in talking to a prospective builder, you sense he is holding something back or there is a hesitation about doing something you want done, dig into it. Once you've committed to an agreement, it's expensive and difficult to get uncommitted.

Competency

When you talk to owners of houses the builder has built, ask if you can go through the houses yourself. You're likely to be more critical than someone who has learned to live with the mistakes the builder made.

- A neighbor moved into a new house and had been living there two or three weeks when I asked how he liked it. "Oh, it's great," he said. Then I told him I was writing a book about things builders do and don't do and asked if I could look through the house. There, in the kitchen, sat a refrigerator next to a set of cupboards at right angles to it. The refrigerator blocked access to the cupboards and the cupboards wouldn't let the freezer door open far enough to get to the internal baskets and ice tray.

Yet, when I knocked on the door and asked what he thought of the house, I got a positive response. It's better to be your own judge, if you can.

Does the prospective builder do his own house design? If he does, re-read the part of Chapter 3 dealing with house designers. It is possible for a builder to be a good designer, but it pays to be skeptical.

Subcontractor Management

Talk to the builder about subcontractor management. Does he know what's good and bad sub work? Does he carefully, usually daily, inspect the work the subs do or does he wait until there's a problem before he gets involved? If he waits for problems, forget the builder. When he spends his time covering up problems that should have been caught in the first place, then he'll also cover up problems that you'll have to live with.

Let the builder know up front that you're going to want to put a lot of things in writing that he's probably not used to. You are going to want the house built the way you want it, which is not necessarily the way his subcontractors have been doing it. If he has trouble with that, have second thoughts. A builder who is good at managing his subs won't have trouble with detailed specifications. He'll welcome them because that means there are a lot of things that have been thought through and won't have to be changed or re-done once construction has started. One who doesn't keep on top of things will have a lot of trouble when you spell out the details and will not be happy about having them in writing.

Visit a work site or two where the builder is putting up houses. Check if there is a lot of construction debris on the site. A good builder won't let this debris accumulate, for two reasons:

• It can be a safety hazard.

• It can get in the way and interfere with the progress of the job.

The Builder as an Advisor

One of the functions which a builder accepts when he signs a contract with you is that he will be your advisor until the house is done. There are just too many details for you to have covered all of them in your specifications. Good counselors and advisers are knowledgeable and have a real desire to do what's best. Beware of the yes man. What you need is good advice, not someone who agrees regardless of what your say.

It's natural for a builder to be biased in his advice. He has his own ax to grind in the building process and it's to be expected that his counsel will swayed by his personal likes and dislikes. Consider his recommendations but on important matters get outside advice from someone else who is knowledgeable and competent.

If you decide not to get competitive bids, remember that you will be working with the builder from the beginning to the end. You will be limited in your choices by his knowledge and yours. This is one reason that you need to learn all you can on your own.

Home Warranties

There are several kinds of warranties the builder may offer you with the house, or there may be none at all. For your own protection, insist on having a copy of the warranty before you commit to the house. The obvious reason is to be sure you know what protection you have before it's too late. Another reason is to see what kind of protection the builder can offer.

For new homes the usual warranty involves three time periods. For the first year the builder is responsible for anything involving materials and workmanship on the house. For the second year the builder himself warrants against major structural defects and defects in the wiring, plumbing, heating, and air conditioning systems. For the next eight years the warranty company pays for fixing these major structural defects.

During the first year the builder or one of the subcontractors will usually fix anything that needs doing immediately. Near the end of the year you should figure on giving your builder a list of the things that need fixing. These include cracking wallboard joints (due to shrinking or warping wood), carpets that need tightening up, loose tile, etc. If your builder gives you a bad time about this, there is an arbitration procedure that can be invoked.

After the first year, you may be surprised to find that the warranted "major structural defect" really means catastrophic failure, like the house falling down. Big cracks in the wallboard, carpet seams that split, tiles that fall off of walls—none of these are "major."

The warranties are usually transferable to new owners.

There are other pluses to these warranties that may be as important as the things they protect. First, the builder has to pass a check by the warranty organization for the insurance to be issued at all. Second, if the builder goes out of business, the warranty company will stand behind the entire obligation so that you aren't left holding the bag.

The Contract

Insist on a contract with all the things you want in writing. Any agreement you reach with a builder should have the blessing of an attorney versed in real estate before you sign it. It's just good insurance.

Include a clause that says all work is to be done in accord with pertinent building codes and that an OK by the local building inspector does not relieve the contractor of this responsibility. This will get around any arguments that might arise if the inspector passes something that's not in accord with code. (And this happens all too often.)

Be sure to have in writing an understanding that you and your architect or house designer can visit the work site at any time and can inspect the work. Include a proviso that says if you find something you don't think is right, you can call the builder and have the problem looked at before the next phase of work starts. If you find something in the first-floor framing that's wrong, don't let them start on the second floor before the problem is fixed, otherwise it may never be fixed. Be prepared to accept, as a part of this proviso, that you'll not interfere with the subcontractors doing their work. The last thing anyone needs is to have a sub walk off of the job because he feels you are hassling him. Watch what's going on, but don't interfere. If you have questions, direct them to the builder.

Make sure your agreement with the builder details the method for making changes in the agreement. Once work starts, most changes will involve additional costs. Sometimes these costs will seem unreasonable to you but remember that the builder has a schedule involving many subcontractors and material suppliers. When you want a change that'll affect that schedule, you cause problems for him. The only recourse he has is to charge you for it. As a minimum, this will include the interest on the construction loan due to a schedule slip.

Put a completion date in the contract with penalties for not making the date. Make sure the penalties are enough to cover you when the date slips. Will you have to be living in a motel and put your furniture in storage? If so, cover yourself. However, expect that any changes you want made in the contract will include a change in the completion date.

Don't expect the builder to work miracles. When he has to depend upon so many subcontractors and suppliers, it is virtually certain that things will not go smoothly from start to finish. A good builder will handle the rough spots as part of the job and will have put some time and money in reserve to handle a reasonable number of unforeseen occurrences. Once he's under contract to you, try to be as cooperative as you can. If you've done a good job in working out just what you want and putting it in writing so there are no misunderstandings, you should be able to stand back and watch it happen.

Chapter 13

Construction Checklist

If subcontractors never did anything wrong, this chapter wouldn't be needed. If builders checked everything the subs did, this chapter wouldn't be needed. But that's not the way the world of building is. Subs sometimes take short cuts, or they don't know better, or they just don't pay any attention to what they're doing. Builders are busy people and, to remain competitive, they don't take the time to check every detail. They check what they have time for and rely on the subs to do their jobs right. It's a calculated risk on their part but it's a part of being in business.

When something isn't done right that the builder doesn't see and do something about, either you catch it or it's in your house forever. Thus, the more you know about what should be done and the more time you spend watching the house under construction, the better the house will be. To the extent that your agreement with your designer or architect calls for them to make site inspections, the amount of time you need to spend will be reduced.

Your contract with your builder will include a catch-all specification to the effect that the workmanship will be to industry standards. This, of course, could be a great source of friction between you and the builder because these industry standards are not clearly defined. Some workmanship seen in looking at new houses was discussed in earlier parts of the book. In this chapter, some more aspects are noted. These, of course, can only touch the surface of what craftsmen can do because of ignorance or misunderstanding or just plain sloppiness. As before, it is suggested that you, insofar as feasible, protect yourself against poor workmanship by including many specific requirements in your specifications.

It was recommended earlier that you keep a close check on what's being done in the house as it's being built; daily, if you can. (An average of 15 minutes per day, some days more, most less, should be enough to keep on top of things.) One purpose for doing this is to catch the workmanship shortcomings right after they occur while they can be fixed without impacting the rest of the house. How you want to handle these with your builder will depend upon the relationship you have with him. You can cover many details in the specifications, but there are a legion more things that can happen that will never be thought of ahead of time.

Check the items listed below and watch for anything else that isn't right. In general, those things covered by the building codes are not in the list because presumably the inspectors will watch these things to protect you. But they are just as prone to error as the rest of us, so keep your eyes open all of the time you are around the job site.

Have an arrangement with the builder about what is to be done when you see something you don't like. The arrangement should be something like: you call him when you see a problem and follow it up with a written note. (Keep a copy of the note and don't hesitate to nudge him if the problem isn't taken care of soon enough that won't cause more problems in later stages of construction.) If it's something critical, you want to be able to say something about it to the subcontractor right then and there.

The list is arranged, more or less, in the order of the phases of building the house so that as time goes on you should be able to just go down the list. Of necessity, the design of the house will impact on when certain pieces of work are done (as, for example, whether the house uses a slab floor or has a crawl space). Or the builder may use a different technique for construction that makes some parts of the list inappropriate (as, for example, when he has walls pre-built away from the site). So use the list as reminders of things to watch for.

Except for a few critical places, you shouldn't expect precision for two reasons: you won't get it and nobody will know the difference anyway. As a general rule if you, as a novice, can see a problem with your naked eye it's probably worth worrying about. The critical places are mentioned below. For the others, look but don't bring your measuring tools unless it is to confirm what you think you see without them.

Site Layout

A first step for the builder is to lay the house out on the lot. For this he (or a sub) will mark where the corners of the house will go and the amount of dirt that has to be removed.

House location. See that the house looks about as it should, both relative to the sides of the lot and above (or below) the street. If you're in doubt, then get out your measuring tape and level. Do look carefully that the house is square on the lot.

Dig Out

The next step is for a sub to dig out for the crawl space under the house or for the slab. This often means having dirt hauled away from the site.

Grading. Check that the area where the house is to go has been properly graded; it should be level unless it has a crawl space and there is a ground water problem. In this case it should be sloped toward one corner where a drain will go.

Foundation Forms

When the forms are all in place awaiting the delivery of concrete is your last chance to check the house's location on the lot, both horizontally and vertically. If you want to check this one, be on your toes. It is not unusual to have the last nail go into the forms while the concrete truck is waiting.

Check squareness. See if square corners look about square. If they don't, out comes the tape measure again. There are two techniques that may be helpful. For any part of the foundation which is rectangular, the two diagonals should be the same length. If they are not, the corners are not square. The other way is to use the 3:4:5 technique.

3:4:5. Start at a corner and measure along one wall, say 6 feet (3 × 2) and along a right-angle wall 8 feet (4 × 2) and make marks. The distance between the marks across the corner should be 10 feet (5 × 2). Or use 9:12:15 or any other multiple of 3:4:5. The longer the measurements, the more accurate the check.

Slab Floors

Level forms. Check if the forms are level. With a slab floor the forms will determine if the whole floor of the house is level.

Pipes. Check the location of the pipes that run through the concrete. If these aren't right, they're not going to be changed once the slab is poured. This is one place where it's probably a good idea to use the tape measure because if the pipes aren't right, it can throw everything off.

Houses with Crawl Spaces

Level forms. Check that forms are level. If they're not, you'll end up with slope in your house.

Piers. Check the placement of the piers, the pieces of concrete in the crawl space that hold up the interior of the house. If these are not put in the right places, the framers will have to do some makeshift corrections which may degrade the physical integrity of the house design. The foundation drawing for the house shows where these piers should be located.

Before the Subfloor Insulation is Installed

This next section doesn't apply where there is a slab floor. In a crawl space the insulation is installed before the subfloor itself is laid over it. Once the insulation is tied into place, it won't be easy to see the gas pipes, water pipes, drains, and heating system ducts without crawling under the house and then it won't be easy for the subcontractors to correct any goofs you might find.

Exterior bibbs. Check that the pipes for exterior hose bibbs are where they are supposed to be. If stop-and-waste valves are used, check that they're located where they will be easily accessible.

Floor joists. If joists are used, take a close look at them. They should not be badly warped, it'll be asking for squeaky floors if they are. Be sure they are firmly fastened in their hangers.

Pipes. Check how water and gas pipes are fastened to the joists or beams under the house. Depending on what you have put in your specifications regarding noise, check that water pipes do not touch joists or beams except where they are anchored. If they go through holes bored in a joist they should not be touching, otherwise they can cause floor squeaks and/or noisy pipes. No pipes should be rubbing against a floor joist or beam.

Check that any water pipes in the crawl space that will be exposed after the floor insulation has been installed are themselves insulated. (Or make a note to check them later.)

Drains. Similarly check clearance of drain and sewer pipes for potential sources for floor squeaks or for noise generation when water is running through them. If your specs call for it, be sure drains are insulated.

Heating ducts. Check that heating ducts will put floor registers where you want them. (There should have been an agreed-upon location for these before work started.)

Check that the duct sizes are in accord with the HVAC plans.

Check that flexible ducts are not collapsed. This is most likely to occur where they go around corners and where they connect to the boot under a floor register but can happen anyplace where someone has banged into them. Since they will generally be completely wrapped with several inches of insulation, you won't be able to see too well. Don't hesitate to put a hand down into the boots and feel that the joint between the boot and the duct has not collapsed.

Crawl space drain. If the plans call for a crawl space drain, check that it is in place. It should be at the lowest place in the crawl space. It should be clear so that any water which might get in the crawl space will be drained.

Visqueen. Check that the Visqueen (plastic sheet) has been laid over all of the crawl space. (This check should be done by the building inspector, but in at least one city they're not very fussy about this. You should insist.)

Post and Beam Construction

After the subfloor deck has been laid but before anything has been put on top of it, take a close look at the deck lumber. What you are looking for here are those things that can reduce the chances of floor squeaks developing.

Warped boards. Look for warped boards. If they're bad, insist on having them taken out. They'll cause an uneven floor. If they're not bad, take a hard look that they've been securely nailed, or preferably screwed, to the beams underneath. You've no way to know if they'll warp some more and, if they do, you want to take every precaution that they won't pull up and become a squeak problem.

When the First Floor Wall Studs Are Up

Now's the time to check if your walls are going to be straight, vertical, and square. If the studs aren't right, nothing else can be.

Openings. Check that door and window openings are where they're supposed to be, including all closets openings.

Electric boxes. Look at the stud arrangements where electrical switch boxes are to go. Be sure that the framers have left room to put the boxes where your specifications say they are to be put.

Medicine cabinets. In bathrooms, check that the framers have put studs in the right places so that medicine cabinets can be installed.

Floor plates. Check if the floor plates are straight (these are the boards that lay on the subfloor or slab to which the studs are nailed.) If they're not straight your walls won't be either. Plates should not be chopped up into several pieces except on long runs; this goes for the top plates as well as the floor plates.

Check that each stud stands flush on the plate. It shouldn't stick out in back or front or it will cause a problem with the wallboard.

Studs. Check the straightness of the studs. Framing lumber is not hand picked so don't expect perfection, but remember that any warps in the front-to-back of studs will result in the same curves in your wall.

Check how vertical the studs are, particularly in the direction where they would cause the wall to lean. Again, don't expect perfection but, unless you want a leaning wall, they'd better not be far off.

Top plates. Check the top plates on walls that they are horizontal. You'll probably need a level for this one. It's difficult to see at this stage whether a piece of wood over your head is level or not.

Pipes. Re-check that pipes which come up into the house from underneath are in the right places, including gas, water, drain and sewer. These will usually be caught, if they're not right, when the plumber gets around to install sinks, basins and fixtures.

Particularly check if the water is there for the refrigerator, this one is too often overlooked.

The Second Floor

The things to look for on the second floor, if there is one, are much the same as the first floor.

Joists. See that no badly warped joists are used and that joists are properly fastened in their hangers.

Pipes. Check between floors that pipes are not touching any floor joists or other framing lumber.

Before Cover Up

All of the work that is installed in the walls will be covered up by insulation or wallboard or both. Before either of these is installed check on electrical work, plumbing, heating ducts and fireplaces.

Electrical Work

Box mountings. Check that outlet and switch electrical boxes stick out in front of the studs by a little less than the thickness of the wallboard to be used. When boxes stick out too far the switch or outlet cover can never be pulled down tight against the wall. When they don't stick out far enough there is a high probability, when the outlet or switch is installed in the box, that the outlet or switch will break down the edge of the wallboard and the outlet or switch won't be straight.

Include telephone jack and TV outlet boxes in your checks. Check that these boxes are the specified distances from the floor.

Check mounting box locations against the plans and specifications. Don't forget lights for halls and stairs.

Check the location of the boxes for telephone jacks. Check that the right kind of wiring was done for the telephones (all jacks in parallel or separate wires from each jack to the interface box, whichever your specification called for).

Check that boxes for TV outlets are all where they are supposed to be. If you have a special interconnection box for TV cables, check that that's in place and that the cables run to it.

Fixtures. Check that 3-conductor wiring is used from fixtures and fans where your specifications call for this.

Check that fixture mounting boxes are what and where they're supposed to be.

Alarm system wiring. If your alarm system is pre-wired or if you have special wiring for a sound system in the house, be sure that's all in place and checked out before it gets covered up with wallboard.

Plumbing

Nail plates. Check that nail plates have been put in place on every stud or plate where there is even a remote chance that a wallboard nail or screw might penetrate the stud and hit a pipe.

Pipes in outside walls. Check that runs of water pipes in outside walls are located as close as possible to the inside of the house.

Heating Ducts

Location. As a final check before the walls are sealed up, double check that heating ducts are where you want them. Check the cold air returns also. As before, double check that there aren't any collapsed ducts anyplace.

Fireplaces

If you have a fireplace, there are two steps in checking it out; before and after it is actually installed. The steps below are for a manufactured metal firebox. Similar steps are appropriate for a brick and mortar unit.

The many kinds of fireplaces make it difficult to come up with anything like a comprehensive checklist but before the wallboard is in place, look the fireplace over carefully.

Before Installation

Insulation. If the fireplace is on an outside wall, check that the wall behind the fireplace has been insulated. If it is a fireplace mounted in a chase, check that bottom of the chase and the ceiling in the chase above the fireplace have been insulated.

Combustion air. If there's supposed to be a combustion air duct, check that it's there and open.

After Installation

Gas Lighter or Gas Logs—If it's a wood-burning fireplace with a gas lighter or if there are to be gas logs:

Connection for gas. Check that the gas is stubbed into the fireplace.

Control valve. Check that the wall valve for turning the gas on and off works easily. (I can attest that they don't always and, once the wallboard is up, you've got a problem.)

Damper (if there is one). Check that it works smoothly and that it stays where it's put. (Again, I can attest that some of them won't stay where you put them. This can cause some pretty smoky times in your house.)

Check that there's some way to know the way the damper is turned without having to crawl into the fireplace and look up the chimney.

Gas Fireplace—If it's a gas fireplace:

Switches. Check that the switch for starting it is where it's supposed to be, not just thrown someplace on the wall. If it's on a wall with other switches, the switch should be in the same electrical box that holds the other switches.

If it's supposed to have a separate fan control (switch or rheostat), see that the control is located where it's supposed to be, presumably with the on-off switch,

Caulking

Caulking is used to fill in the inevitable cracks left after the various phases of construction. These can occur in the exterior siding and around holes cut in exterior walls particularly at doors and windows.

Joints. Each butt joint in siding should be caulked.

Windows. Caulking should be used liberally around window frames to seal against air infiltration. This must be checked before any window wrapping is done because the wrapping will cover up uncaulked cracks without sealing them.

Doors. Similarly, look around exterior doors after the door frames have been installed but before the trim is in place.

Around pipes, ducts and wires. Where pipes or ducts go into un-
heated space, like the attic or the crawl space, the holes around
them should be caulked. Similarly, for electric wiring.

After the Wallboard Is Up and Taped

Try to make this check before the wallboard is textured and painted,
otherwise if you find something it may be difficult to fix without
the wallboard looking patched.

Nails and screws. There should be no nails or screws showing
anyplace.

Around electrical boxes. Look carefully around electrical boxes,
those used for switches, outlets and fixtures. The holes in the
wallboard should be just big enough for the boxes but no bigger. If they are too large, then the covers won't cover them and
you'll end up with unsightly holes in your wall.

Mudding. Be sure the wallboard is finished far enough down on
the wall so that whatever baseboards you are using, if any, will
cover the seam between the wallboard and the floor.

Check the mudding at outside corners. Is the wall straight
enough that there will be no gaps when baseboards are
installed?

Look at inside corners. They should not be rounded but go
squarely back into the corner.

Wallpapering. If you have walls that are to be wallpapered, be sure
they are very clearly marked that they are not to be textured or
painted. (It's a lot harder to get the texturing off of a wall than
it is to put it on. In fact, the easiest way to fix a goof like this is
to put more mud on so that you end up with a smooth surface
for the wallpaper.)

If the wallpaper or trim is going all the way to the ceiling, check
that the joint where the wall meets the ceiling is straight—otherwise the top edge of the paper will look uneven.

Wallboard Finishing

Workmanship. Look over the texturing to see that it's what you
wanted and to see if it's uniform.

Check painting for thin or missed areas. In darker hall areas you may need extra light to see this.

Check that the paint is the right color.

Woodwork

Painted woodwork. Be sure that all cracks and seams were filled before they were painted.

Stained and lacquered. Check that corners are tight and snug. There should be no places where there are gaps due to sloppy workmanship. The finish should be smooth and even. Watch for missed or thin spots.

Look at moldings where nail holes are filled. The finish should be uniform all around the nail holes; there should be no difference in the finish caused by improperly applied putty.

Look for dents in the woodwork. The pieces should be replaced; you can't fix them, ever.

Cabinets

Some of this can be checked at the cabinetmaker's if he is local and you can time it right.

Interior corners. Look where sides and back meet. These should be tight.

Door alignment. Look for warped doors, there shouldn't be any. Try opening the doors and letting them go. They should close smoothly and without banging.

Check that doors fit okay and that they're adjusted so that bottoms of doors on adjacent cupboards are even.

Spaces between doors should be even from top to bottom. (Most hinges allow some alignment of doors at any time. This is usually done when the cabinets are installed.)

Finish. Check the finish carefully for dents or banged-up spots. Check that the finish is even. If the finish work was done on site, check for the presence of dust particles embedded in the finish. There should be no runs anyplace including shelves and drawer bottoms.

Finger grooves and pulls. If there are finger grooves, check that they are on the top or bottom of the drawers as called for by the specification.

Are pulls what you specified?

Slide hardware. Check that pull-out shelves do not leave the slide hardware exposed where it can scratch the insides of cabinet doors.

Check that all drawers and pull-out shelves operate smoothly.

Mounting. Check that mounting screws are covered if called for by the specification.

Check that the trim pieces on sides and tops of cabinets are snugly in place and do not leave unsightly gaps.

Be sure that the stick-on rubber bumpers on doors have been installed so that doors don't bang when closed.

Appliances

Models. Check that all appliances, including the water heater(s), are what you specified.

Operability. Check that each of the appliances functions properly.

HVAC

Model. Check that the furnace, air conditioner and/or the heat pump are what you specified or agreed to with the builder and the mechanical subcontractor.

Operability. Run each of these through it's cycles to check that they are working properly.

Thermostat. Check that it appears to be functioning properly. (You'll get a better check after you move in.)

Instruction Manuals

Check that all of the instruction manuals for the appliances, HVAC equipment, and water heater are there.

The Exterior

Concrete Work

Location. Before any concrete is to be poured, you should check that the forms are where they are supposed to be.

Pipes and conduits. If pipes or conduits are to go under the concrete, be sure they're in place and that the ends of them stick well outside of where the concrete will be.

Finish. If you can be present at the pour, be sure that the appropriate finish is used.

Roof

It shouldn't necessary to climb on the roof to check it out; in fact, if it isn't architectural composition or asphalt shingles, you probably shouldn't anyway. A pair of binoculars will help.

Concrete, terra cotta, or shake. Look for broken pieces.

Composition or asphalt shingle. Check that it all lays flat; sometimes nails or staples aren't driven all the way down and these hold up the row on top. When not flat, rain can be driven under the shingles or, in a worst case, wind can catch them and tear them off the house.

Nooks and crannies. Look for places that birds could use as a nest. If you had not specified that these be blocked, then plan on doing it yourself.

Flashings. Look around the flashings where pipes come up through the roof. Everything should be snug and flat. This is particularly important because leaks here may not be noticed for a long time and a large amount of insulation in the attic can be soppy wet (and ruined) before any water shows up in the house.

Ridges. Check that all of the roofing pieces along roof ridges have been put in place.

Gutters. Look at the gutters and see that they are all snugly nailed to the fascias. If they are painted, check this.

Soffits. Check eave soffits. If they are boxed in, was the job done neatly without unsightly gaps? Is everything painted?

Downspouts and drains. Check downspouts and drains to the street. Make sure they are open and fit firmly so that water won't come gushing back out of them in a heavy downpour.

Siding

Caulking. Look around the house. Are there any gaps? Is everything caulked that should be?

Nails. Are there any nails that need pounding down?

Paint. Is everything painted the right color? Is the paint on evenly, no misses and no runs?

Lights with lap siding. If lap siding is used, check that any exterior lights are mounted vertically rather than following the contour of the siding. (This should have been take care of before the siding was installed.)

Deck

If you have a deck, check that it was made according to plan. If there is gas for your barbecue, check that it wasn't covered up when the deck was built. Check that there are steps down from the deck if they are required.

Grading

The last step, after the house is finished, is to do the finish grading. This should leave the lot as shown in the site plan.

Slope. The dirt should slope away from the house and there should be no low spots that will collect water. If you had some special requirements in your specifications, check that they were taken care of.

Tracer Wires

In Oregon, the Uniform Plumbing Code has been amended to require that color-coded tracer wires be put in the ground with any nonmetallic water, sewer and gas lines running from the street to your house. These wires make it possible to trace the location of these pipes under dirt or concrete so that, if any digging is to be done on your lot, the exact location of the pipes can be known before work starts. (The same wires are used on the pipes under the street.)

You should check in your state to see if they have similar requirements. If they do, then check where these pipes enter your house; the wires should be in plain sight above the finished grade, meaning above the dirt or concrete. If you can't find them, talk to the builder or the plumbing inspector.)

Afterword

Here are three books dealing with building a custom house that you may find useful:

- H.L.Kibbey, *How to Finance a Home in the Pacific Northwest*, 2nd ed., (Lake Oswego, OR: Panoply Press, 1993), 230 pages.

  This book deals with all aspects of financing a home. Chapter 24, in particular, is a discussion of financing for custom homes. (Don't be put off by the regional title of this book. Its contents are applicable everywhere.)

- Jim Locke, *The Well-Built House*, rev. ed., (Boston, MA: Houghton Mifflin Co., 1992), 302 pages.

  The author is a builder and the book delves into the nuts and bolts of building your home from that perspective. It includes a heavy dosage of the author's personal likes and dislikes.

- Douglas Hedlund, *What Every Potential Homeowner Should Know About Construction*, Vol.1, (Tucson, AZ: Condata Company, 1989), 156 pages.

  An even more detailed look at construction details. Also by a builder but offered in a non-judgmental way.

You now have a better idea of what we meant when we said, "Nobody said it wasn't work." But you can start down the road with a lot more confidence about how to get a user-friendly home without worrying so much about all of the things you might forget. The tasks of finding a designer, getting a set of plans and specifications, selecting a builder, and seeing the house being built will be a lot less formidable.

Part V

Appendices and Glossary

CC&Rs
Building Codes
Refrigerators
GFCI Protection
Fireplaces
Telephone and Television Wiring
Builders' Associations
Real Estate People
Exhaust Systems
Cabinets
Countertops
Ceiling Fans
Heat Pumps
Glossary

CC&Rs

"Covenants, Conditions, and Restrictions" are legal conditions that apply to a piece of real property. They are tied to the deed and tell the owner what things may and may not be done with the property.

Purpose

CC&Rs are used to provide for a continuing control over what people can do on lots in a subdivision. CC&Rs are generally beneficial. They are a legal means to protect you from the boor who doesn't care what his house or lot looks like and, makes the whole neighborhood look seedy, thus ruining both your way of life and the value of your property.

What CC&Rs Mean to You

People who have lived with CC&Rs that provide for controls in the subdivision after the subdivider has gone will almost always prefer to buy in another subdivision with the same kind of CC&Rs. While they make the neighborhood a better place to live for most owners, there are a few to whom the CC&Rs are a continual source of irritation and frustration. These are the people who have their own ideas about what they are going to do on their property. It is important that you know about what's in this legal document before you make any decisions about a piece of property; you may want to find a place with tighter controls or you may not want to live with what's there already.

The title company will require that you sign a statement to the effect that you have read the CC&Rs before they will issue you a deed for your new home. Don't let it get that far. BEFORE YOU

PUT A PENNY DOWN ON A PIECE OF PROPERTY READ THE CC&Rs. At first they may seem like just another piece of the red tape but that document is legally binding whether you read it or not.

My wife was an officer on the board of directors of a large, strong homeowners' association and she'll tell you she couldn't believe the number of people who were unable to understand how someone could make them take down their TV antenna, repaint their house, or water their shrubbery. It's their property and no one can tell them what they can and cannot do on it, right? Absolutely wrong. If it's in the CC&Rs, it's binding. There may be some surprises although usually not of such a substantial nature as to make you want to back off. The realtor or seller with whom you are dealing can get a copy for you.

The term CC&R may not be an exact abbreviation for many of these documents. I have one titled "DECLARATION OF COVENANTS, CONDITIONS, RESTRICTIONS, ASSESSMENTS, CHARGES, SERVITUDES, LIENS, RESERVATIONS, and EASEMENTS!" However, when you say CC&Rs people will know what you mean.

Here's a list of the most commonly seen items in some 25 CC&Rs that were reviewed: easements, occupant age, street parking, driveway parking, home businesses, initial landscaping, antennas of any kind, nuisances, maintenance, mailboxes and newspaper receptacles, roofing materials, buildings, animals, trash and refuse, blocking of views, temporary buildings, sunshades, awnings, basketball backstops, flagpoles, lights, drilling and mining, party walls and fences, clothes lines, wood piles, and outside storage areas.

CC&Rs come in all flavors and sizes. Some are only two or three pages long and others may be over 60. They are written to cover many things. The first thing they all do is to protect the land developer or subdivider for as long as he has an interest in the subdivision. This protection is to insure that someone who buys a lot does nothing that may cause a drop in the value of the unsold lots.

When the lots are all sold and the subdivider is gone, what then? That depends on what the CC&Rs say. The simplest ones say nothing. Others include the formation of a homeowners' association which can go on forever.

For the simplest CC&Rs, any benefits that may accrue to the homeowners are coincidental. The subdivider maintains architectural control over what may be put on a lot, but it applies only until he sells the last lot and is out of there. There may be statements in these CC&Rs about the maintenance of drainage easements, for example, but no means to enforce them after the subdivider is gone, except in a court of law. These kinds of CC&Rs are the easy way out for the land developer, but beware, when you are buying a house in one of these subdivisions, that they offer little protection once the developer is gone.

Even without a homeowners' association, CC&Rs can serve a useful purpose. If someone is about to do something which is not in keeping with the CC&Rs, an owner can threaten to sue the offender. Simply the threat of the suit will often be enough to bring the offender into line. However, unless the offense is really gross or the suing homeowner is really sensitive, this will not usually happen because it would not be worth the cost and hassle. If it exists, the homeowners' association is the better vehicle to insist on enforcement.

CC&Rs can be amended or even deleted. How this is done should be in the CC&Rs themselves. Commonly it takes a ⅔ or ¾ majority of the lot owners although in one CC&R this was a simple majority with the proviso that the Declarant (a.k.a. the developer) has the right of veto over any amendment.

Homeowners' Associations

Purpose

When a new subdivision is planned, there is frequently something associated with the subdivision which is unique to it and which will require maintenance over the years. An entrance which is signed, painted and landscaped will require attention and the homeowners' association is the appropriate organization to take the responsibility to have this done. There may be streets, common recreational areas, swimming pools, parks, RV parks, and even golf courses which are owned and maintained by the homeowners' association.

A primary purpose of a homeowners' association is to provide for the upkeep of these areas which are owned in common by the homeowners (the common area).

But it doesn't stop there. The developer, in an effort to make the subdivision unique, may have adopted a theme for the subdivision. He will write the CC&Rs to be sure that everyone who buys and builds will maintain that theme.

Organization

Homeowners' associations are usually non-profit corporations. Some CC&Rs spell out in detail the make-up of the board of directors. Others say little, putting all of the detail into the Articles of Incorporation, a document which is filed with the state when the association is formed. If the CC&Rs don't say just how the board is to be elected and how long the developer is to control it, you should get a copy of the Articles of Incorporation. Again, the realtor or seller should be able to get these for you from the land developer. Eventually you may want to get a copy of the by-laws for the association. This is not a legally recorded document, but it can tell you about the internal organization and operation of the association.

There is always a certain amount of administrative or management effort involved in running the association; collecting dues, answering questions, writing letters to recalcitrant owners, making arrangements for maintenance work, getting legal help, etc. There are organizations who specialize in this kind of administrative work. You can check to see just what arrangements have been made by the homeowners' association in the subdivision which you are considering, both for association management and for the legal counsel which any association should have.

Homeowners' associations are usually organized to be governed by a board of directors who are elected by the homeowners. Until the developer no longer has an interest in the subdivision, he usually maintains control of the board of directors, frequently by assigning himself more votes than he gives the homeowners. The exact time when control of the board of directors is turned over to the homeowners may be when the developer has sold all or most of the lots or it may be on a pre-determined date or some combination of these.

Homeowners' associations generally have the responsibility to do those things needed to maintain the attractiveness of the subdivision and, in so doing, they can go a long way toward maintaining the aesthetics of the neighborhood and the value of the property. The association usually has, as a subsidiary group, an architectural review committee (or variously, architectural committee or architectural control committee). With a strong set of CC&Rs, the association, through the architectural review committee, can keep a tight rein on anything which could damage property values. The architectural review committee is usually given the responsibility to promulgate a set of "architectural guidelines" about many of the details which require review. These also spell out the process for getting the requisite prior approval for virtually anything you may want to do on the outside of your house.

Costs

All of this does not come free. Homeowner association dues may run from less than $20 to upward of $200 per month. If this financial burden seems too onerous for the benefits that you would receive, then it would better to find a subdivision where the CC&Rs make no provision for an on-going homeowners' association. (As noted later, you may find you have two homeowners' associations to support. So be sure you know all the facts before you invest.)

Besides the monthly dues to the homeowners' association(s), you may also be subject to special assessments when there is something 'special' that has to be done, such as repaving streets or completely renovating the swimming pool.

Enforcement

What happens if you don't pay your dues or assessments? The homeowners' association can file a lien against your property and either foreclose to get their money or get it, with interest, from the escrow company when you sell the house.

You will find that CC&Rs provide for penalties when the homeowner does not comply with the CC&Rs themselves or with the guidelines issued by the architectural review committee. The penalties frequently involve allowing the homeowners' association to correct the deficiency and assessing a lien against the property to cover the cost of the work along with administrative and legal fees. It is then handled just as with unpaid dues, i.e., either by foreclosure or by taking the money from escrow when the house is sold (or the owner can pay the costs to the association at any time).

All of the legal terms in the world won't mean a thing unless they are enforced. As long as the subdivider is around, he will take some interest in protecting his investment. Sometimes he may need some prodding when a property owner does something which definitely should not be done, but as long as the developer is looking out for his own self interests you have some modicum of assurance that the CC&Rs will be enforced.

• Don't be too sanguine about this, however. When we moved into our new house in Salem, the developer still had architectural control, including colors of houses. He paid little attention to this responsibility. For a new house on our block, the builder chose a ghastly shade of green. The developer's attitude was, "If it's too bad, it won't sell and the builder will have to repaint it." In this case the developer was right. It didn't sell and it was repainted. However, the developer's cavalier attitude did little to assure us that we had any protection from the CC&Rs at all.

With homeowners' associations, things can be different. Loosely written CC&Rs, however, may make it difficult for an association to insist on adherence to the rules. Sometimes, and this is difficult to foresee, the owners will not really be interested in keeping up the neighborhood. It is not unusual for the authority to be there, but to find that the owners themselves do not want to be constrained by the CC&Rs and, by tacit mutual agreement, do not enforce them. (You could always take the homeowners' association to court to make them do their job, but that's so costly that virtually no one will ever do it.)

Association Authority

Some people get particularly irritated by a provision found in many CC&Rs; the "right of entry." This provides that a member of the board of directors or of the architectural review committee may, from time to time, enter onto any lot in the subdivision to see if there is compliance with the requirements of the CC&Rs and/or of the architectural guidelines. And this can be done without the approval of the homeowner!

The homeowners' association and/or the architectural review committee is usually empowered to issue variances to rules or guidelines which cause a hardship in unusual cases. For example, if you have a drainage problem which cannot be fixed until dry weather comes, you could reasonably expect to be granted a variance with regard to when your landscaping has to be put in.

Subassociations

In very large subdivisions, it is not unusual to find you have two sets of CC&Rs with which to deal. The primary subdivider makes up the overall set of CC&Rs for the total subdivision and then sells large parcels of the subdivision to builder/developers who, in turn, will have a set of CC&Rs which apply only to these parcels. The resulting second homeowners' association is known as a subassociation. With all of this go two sets of common areas, two boards of directors, two levels of protection, and two sets of constraints and restrictions. In these cases, there will usually be only one architectural review committee, from the primary subdivider's CC&Rs, that will control most of the things about which you will be concerned.

Guidelines

Once in a great while you will run across a subdivider/developer who is as concerned about your understanding of the CC&Rs as you are. When you are interested in a home or lot in his subdivision, you will get, from him or from the realtor, a set of 'guidelines' which explain in non-legal terms what's in the CC&Rs and in the architectural guidelines and what they mean to the homeowners. With such guidelines you don't have to struggle through all of the legal verbiage in the CC&Rs to find those things which are pertinent to you, the potential homeowner. They can also be comforting in that you then know, in terms you can understand, just what controls there are to maintain the appearance of your neighborhood and the value of your property.

Look for these guidelines and, when you are lucky enough to find them, you will be pleasantly surprised to find that there is, indeed, a developer who is seriously thinking about the importance of the CC&Rs and what they should mean to you.

Building and Energy Codes

Building Codes

Building codes are a real can of worms! To begin with, "building codes" can refer to the whole body of codes in general, or it can refer specifically to one part of that body, the codes about buildings themselves. There are model codes which are used entirely or in part for state codes. These state codes, in turn, may be amended by local governments. The result is that even from one locality to another in the same state there may be differing requirements. The freedom that local governments have to amend or adopt their own codes differs from state to state.

There are codes for each of these areas:

- Building
- Plumbing
- Mechanical (heating, air conditioning, etc.)
- Electrical
- Energy

There are no model energy codes but California, Oregon, Washington, and probably other states have generated extensive energy codes of their own.

The most commonly used model codes are the Uniform Building Code, Uniform Plumbing Code, Uniform Mechanical Code, Uniform Fire Code, and the National Electrical Code.

These model codes cover a wide range of uses: warehouses, apartments houses, single-family homes, manufacturing facilities, stores, office buildings, etc. In the early 1970s another group was formed whose purpose was to come up with a simplified set of codes dedicated specifically to detached one- or two-family dwellings. This group, The Council of American Building Officials (CABO), publishes its own model code that incorporates parts of the other codes. It is intended to be used as the model for state and local codes.

All of these codes are revised periodically, usually every three years. Each state or local code body, in turn, takes the model codes and makes their own set of amendments to them. Thus every state or local jurisdiction have codes which are similar to each other but are different in some areas. From the time a model code is changed until it goes through the inevitable red tape to become a part of a state or local code takes from three to five years.

Sound confusing? It is. Builders and specialists have specific codes that apply to what they do. Since the codes are revised from time to time, it's easy for the electrician, say, to get confused about what's code and what's simply local practice. And this does happen.

The National Electrical Code

In most states, electricians must be licensed to work at their trade. This requires training and passing state tests. All their work has to be inspected by a local building inspector.

Electricians and building inspectors can and do take liberties with the National Electrical Code (NEC). It's something like speed limit laws. We're all licensed drivers. We have police whose job is to enforce the speed limits. So we all drive at 55 or 65 mph which is the posted limit. Ha! What few police there are go after the gross violators and there is a tacit understanding that you don't have to meet the letter of the law. Electricians and building inspectors have similar understandings.

- The local code enforcement office told me that the 20A circuits in the garage and on the deck of our house don't need GFCI protection and that only one of the garage 15A circuits needs it. This is NOT what the NEC says. My new house was not wired according to code.

The National Electric Code is used as the basis for local codes. It spells out in some detail those things the electrician must do when wiring a house. The two thrusts of the code are fire and personal safety. The code does nothing to make the electrical system easier for the home user to use. That's up to the builder, his electrical sub-contractor, and you.

A word of caution about the NEC. Of all of the building codes, this one is probably more frequently violated, and more frequently mis-understood, than any other. I ran across an example of an electrician ascribing code status to what is a local wiring custom. This same lack of knowledge but insistence that it's "code" is also prevalent among suppliers of electrical building materials. If there's any question in your mind, check it out yourself. It's much easier for someone to say that it is or isn't 'code' than to take the time to get out the book.

Energy Codes

Energy conservation has reached such importance in new construction that a new group of codes has evolved to deal with it. There are no model codes in this area so each state does its own thing. A brief look at the similarities and the differences in the codes follows. But first, there are couple of technical terms that should be mentioned.

Insulation Values

Floors, walls, and ceiling of all new construction must be insulated. There are two terms which describe the effectiveness of insulation: R-value and U-value. They are reciprocals, i.e., R=1/U and U=1/R. R-values are used to describe the insulating quantities of materials used under floors and in walls and ceilings. U-values are used to describe the heat loss through windows, skylights, and doors. Actual building heat-loss calculations are performed by summing up the U-values of the various contributors to heat loss.

Tightness

A major source of heat loss is through holes in walls and around doors and windows. To minimize this loss, houses are made tighter and tighter as time goes on. When buildings are made too tight, there is little air exchange with the outside and people in the building breathe the same air over and over. Eventually this can lead to nausea, headaches, and other complaints.

It's also a major headache for energy conservation specialists. On the one hand we don't want to lose heat and on the other hand, if we don't change the air in the house, people may get sick. There's no good way to measure when the air gets unhealthy. The solutions to this dilemma are based on experience and observations, not on hard data such as the amount of carbon dioxide or contaminants in the air. In other words, the whole process is very imprecise.

One approach is to ignore it and assume that there are enough ways for fresh air to get into the house. After all, every time you open a door or a window you get fresh air.

A second approach is to dictate the use of windows that are deliberately made with holes around them and then to use an exhaust fan to force the old air out and pull fresh air in around the windows.

A third approach is to use an air-to-air heat exchanger. A fan in this unit pulls air from the house and exhausts it. This draws outside air into the house through another part of the exchanger. The unit takes some of the heat out of the air that is being exhausted and uses this heat to warm the incoming air. These units typically recover about 35 percent of the energy that was used to heat the air in the first place; the other 65 percent is gone. (But that 35 percent is a whole lot more than the nothing that is salvaged with the vented-window approach.)

The State Codes

Individual states attack the energy conservation problem in widely varying ways. The three that are discussed here give three different approaches. Your state may not have any specific energy conservation codes and may depend upon the insulation requirements in their building codes to take care of the needs for the state.

Washington and California have separate codes dealing with energy conservation and Oregon has added an extensive amendment to the CABO code that covers just energy. The Washington and California codes apply to all buildings; the Oregon amendment discussed here applies only to one- and two-story residential buildings. The underlying idea of these codes is two-fold: 1) energy savings in general and 2) by spending money to build houses which are energy efficient, the homeowner will save money in the long run.

Washington divides the state into two climatic zones, with different insulation requirements for the two zones. Requirements are significantly tougher for houses heated by electricity directly. Washington addresses the question of house tightness in much more detail than do the other states.

Oregon codes don't consider the differences in climate in the different parts of the state. Nor are there distinctions in insulation requirements because of the method of heating the house. Air quality and ventilation are not addressed in the Oregon codes. Oregon requires that fireplaces be capable of getting combustion air from outside the building. (However this is done in a way that gives lip service to the problem but doesn't solve it.)

California divides the state into 16 different climatic zones, each with its own set of requirements. California's codes include concern with the energy taken for air conditioning. Houses heated directly with electricity have their own set of insulation requirements. Air quality and ventilation are not a part of the energy code except that one of the optional calculation packages includes the effects of air infiltration and of air-to-air heat exchangers. The question of heat loss via fireplace flues is addressed in some detail. (See also comments in Appendix E regarding fireplaces and heat loss.)

Some Plumbing Code Notes

The 1991 Uniform Plumbing Code (UPC) allows water piping inside a house to be either copper or chlorinated polyvinyl chloride (CPVC). However, not all states use the UPC for the state plumbing codes or they significantly modify the UPC. In fact, the three west coast states have different codes concerning water pipe and all are different from the UPC. In particular, California doesn't allow any plastic pipe. In Oregon, polybutylene (PB) and cross-linked polyethylene (PEX) are okay as well as CPVC and copper. In Washington, PB is often used.

The main argument against plastic pipes is that they haven't been in use long enough to ensure that they won't cause trouble in the future. Not all states agree with this assessment, obviously.

Note: CPVC and PB are not to be used in hot water systems, PEX is okay for this.

Copper is the material of choice for most plumbing subcontractors. Installing copper takes some skills with soldering joints. CPVC installations can be done by anyone. Copper isn't without its problems, however. In southern California there have been reports of pin hole leaks in copper pipe presumably due to the chemical makeup of the water. California may need to allow plastic piping inside residences to avoid this problem.

CPVC is similar to PVC, the white plastic pipe used in lawn irrigation systems. Unlike PVC, CPVC doesn't soften when used for hot water. CPVC is 15 to 25 percent less expensive than copper. The installation times for the two materials is similar when done by an experienced installer.

Polybutylene and cross-linked polyethylene pipes are similar in that they come in rolls and require special fittings which are neither soldered nor cemented but are strictly mechanical in nature. These fittings must be approved by the building officials. In general, when plumbers use these types of pipe they avoid the use of elbows and couplings by taking advantage of the flexibility and the length of the tubing. This allows single uncut pieces of pipe to go all the way from the manifold to the faucets.

Because there is only one faucet per line coming from the manifold, turning on a second faucet has little impact on the flow to one already running. Thus, if you are taking a shower and someone turns on a faucet someplace else, there will not be the same noticeable impact on either the amount or the temperature of your shower water.

Code Enforcement

Following are addresses and phone numbers for questions about codes in three states that have state agencies:

- California

  Energy—California Energy Commission, (916) 654–5200
  Other—California Department of Housing and Community
     Development, (916) 445–9471

- Oregon Building Code Agency, (503) 378–4133

- Washington State Building Code Council, (206) 586–3423

Arizona, Idaho, and Nevada have no statewide agencies. If you live in states like these, you'll have to be satisfied with the local building department.

A word of understanding and caution regarding building officials and inspectors. These are governmental positions and a certain amount of "politics" is involved in many of the decisions they make. In most areas the building industry is pretty well organized and can bring considerable pressure to bear on building officials and inspectors. The codes, unlike statutes, have not had the benefit of years of judicial decisions backing up what's written. Building officials and inspectors have to make judgments about how far to go in enforcing the letter of the code. Thus we see times when the inspectors will let things pass that aren't in strict compliance with the codes.

State laws differ, of course, but note that building officials and inspectors are liable for their decisions and are occasionally sued for not doing their job right. Generally you will find them to be cooperative.

Refrigerators in Kitchen Layouts

The location of the refrigerator in the kitchen is important in a user-friendly home. It should be placed where using it does not cause extra steps. You should be able to open all of the doors well past straight out so that internal bins and trays can be removed. You should not have to walk around an open door. You should be able to stand in front of the refrigerator, take things out of it and have a place to set them without moving your feet.

In many kitchens the refrigerator location does not meet these criteria, at least not for all common refrigerator configurations. Refrigerators are not a minor cost item. When the day comes for you to sell, you will find that people will dig in their heels about having to buy a new refrigerator just to buy your house. It is important, therefore, not to devalue your home by having a refrigerator location which is not suitable for all refrigerators. And don't forget that you may want to update your own refrigerator someday and you should make sure that changing from a freezer-over model to a side-by-side, or vice versa, is feasible.

These considerations are the subject of this appendix, starting with refrigerator configurations and sizes and including a number of good and bad kitchen arrangements.

Refrigerator Configurations

All refrigerators have a separate freezer compartment. The location of the freezer gives rise to the terms "freezer-under," "freezer-over" and "side-by-side."

Freezer-Under and Freezer-Over Models

In freezer-under models the freezer is a pull-out unit the full width of the refrigerator.

In freezer-over models the freezer is behind a hinged door the full width of the refrigerator. Both the freezer and main doors swing from the same side.

The concerns here are the problems that occur when doors are opened and, in this respect, both freezer-under and freezer-over models have the same potential. To simplify the discussions, they are grouped together and called freezer-over in the rest of the appendix. Don't forget, however, that the discussions apply equally to both.

Side-by-Side Models

In side-by-side units the two sections of the refrigerator mount vertically with separate doors, the freezer being on the left when facing the refrigerator.

Doors

In all units, the doors include shelves, some much deeper than others. On most refrigerators the hinges are arranged so that, when they are opened straight out, the fronts of the doors are aligned with the sides of the unit. In a few of the largest refrigerators hinges are mounted differently and a significant part of the rather thick doors swings out past the side of the box.

The configurations considered here are:

1. Side-by-side units with doors that are even with the side of the refrigerator when they are opened straight out,

2. Side-by-side units with doors that extend past the side of the refrigerator when they are opened straight out,

3. Freezer-over (or freezer-under) units with doors that are hinged on the left side of the unit, and

4. Freezer-over (or freezer-under) units with doors that are hinged on the right side of the unit.

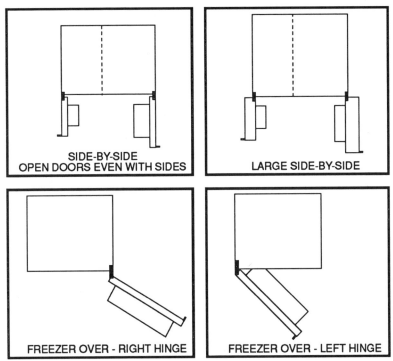

Four different refrigerator configurations.

Refrigerator Sizes

When looking at refrigerators in appliance stores, one gets the definite impression that manufacturers try to outdo each other to make a unit that is a different size than any that has existed before. The dimensions listed here are the result of a survey of a large number of units. Undoubtedly some exist which do not fall in the ranges listed. Use the lists as a guide. Most dimensions will be within the values given. We have divided refrigerators into four groups:

Side-by-side units: 25 to 27 cubic feet

Height	68¾	to	70½	inches (includes hinges)
Width	35¼	to	36	inches
Body depth	27½	to	29¾	inches (not including doors)
Overall depth	31¾	to	36¾	inches (including handles)
Door thickness	2¼	to	4⅝	inches (not including shelves)
Door shelf depth	5¼	to	6½	inches

Side-by-side units: 22 to 24 cubic feet

Height	68¾	to	70½	inches (includes hinges)
Width	35¼	to	36	inches
Body depth	28¼	to	29	inches (not including doors)
Overall depth	31	to	32½	inches (including handles)
Door thickness	2	to	2¼	inches (not including shelves)
Door shelf depth	6	to	6½	inches

Freezer-over units: 20 to 22 cubic feet

Height	66⅝	to	66¾	inches (includes hinges)
Width	31	to	32¾	inches
Body depth	26⅝	to	28½	inches (not including doors)
Overall depth	31½	to	32⅞	inches (including handles)
Door thickness	2¼	to	3½	inches (not including shelves)
Door shelf depth	6½	to	6¾	inches

Freezer-over unit: 13 cubic feet

Height	60	inches (includes hinges)
Width	28	inches
Body depth	23¼	inches (not including doors)
Overall depth	31½	inches (including handles)
Door thickness	2½	inches (not including shelves)
Door shelf depth	6½	inches

Refrigerator Placement

With shelves mounted on the doors of all refrigerators, it is necessary to open the doors well past straight out in order to pull the interior bins out of the refrigerator. Since these will need to be removed for cleaning from time to time, it is important that doors be capable of opening as far as they're designed to. This is approximately 150 degrees, not all the way around to the side but well past straight out front.

For side-by-side freezer doors, this ability to open fully is also needed for access to the ice-cube storage area.

Put simply, THERE SHOULD NEVER BE ANYTHING NEXT TO A REFRIGERATOR WHICH RESTRICTS HOW FAR THE DOORS CAN OPEN.

Refrigerators Next to Walls

As can be seen from the tables, depths of bodies of refrigerators (excluding the 13 cu. ft. unit) run from 25 to 30 inches. Allowing 2 inches at the rear for water and electrical connections, the distance from the back wall to the front of the units, excluding doors, is about 27". If there is a wall longer than this beside the unit, one of two things will happen: either the door won't open fully or the refrigerator cannot be placed all the way back in the space allocated for it.

With freezer-over models the doors could be hinged on the side away from the wall to avoid this problem. There are two objections to this:

1. You would have to walk around such a door every time you use the refrigerator and

2 . When a side-by-side unit is placed there, one of its doors won't open past straight out.

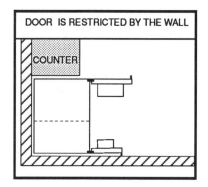

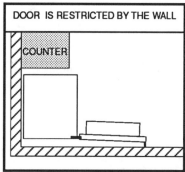

Refrigerators against walls
are always bad news.

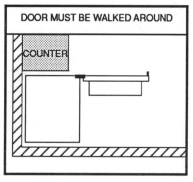

The safest thing is to go with a kitchen plan in which the refrigerator does not have a wall on either side. Most modern-day plans are like this, but not all.

• In Tracy, California a furnished model was seen in which the refrigerator was stuck up against the wall between the kitchen and the dining room. Even though the decorator had scrambled to downplay the problem by putting a smaller than normal freezer-over refrigerator in the allocated space, the door could not be opened far enough to get the meat or vegetable bin out.

This arrangement will force the home user to pull the refrigerator out into the middle of the kitchen for cleaning.

Swinging the doors on the other side would permit them to open but then it would be necessary to walk around the doors to get to the rest of the kitchen.

It's not a user-friendly arrangement.

Refrigerators Next to Doors

A fairly common arrangement is to put the refrigerator beside the wall that has the door into the dining room. This may allow the doors to swing open farther but it doesn't solve the problem. If the wall beside the refrigerator is long, then the doors cannot be opened.

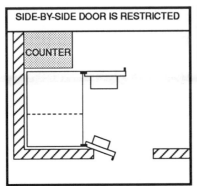 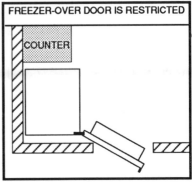

Refrigerators against walls with doors aren't any better.

If the wall is shorter or the refrigerator is moved forward, then the freezer-over doors will hit the opposite side of the doorway and side-by-side units will stick some 3" to 6" (including the handles) out into the doorway. Neither is user-friendly.

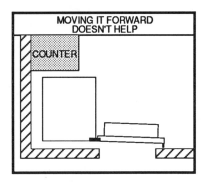

Refrigerators beside doors
just don't work.

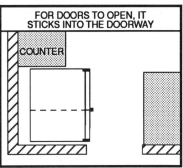

Refrigerators Next to Right-Angle Counters

There are worse kitchens than those which put the refrigerator
against a wall! In these, there is a right-angle counter right beside
the refrigerator. Now not only will the freezer door of the user's
side-by-side refrigerator not open but the cabinet drawer and door
under the counter will also open only a little ways, making the whole
back end of the under-counter cabinet virtually useless.

A refrigerator should never
be alongside a counter.

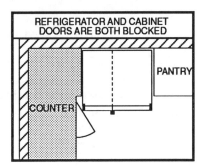

Some User-Friendly Refrigerator Placements

Walls used to cover the side of the refrigerator for aesthetic reasons are okay as long as they don't interfere with the doors.

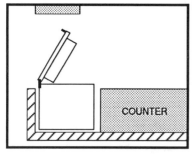 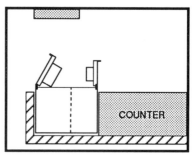

A small wall beside a refrigerator is fine.

Putting the refrigerator next to a pantry, a broom closet, or cabinet-mounted ovens works out fine, too, because nothing then interferes with the full swing of the doors.

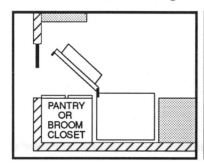 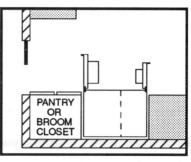

Keep the refrigerator away from a doorway to avoid door problems.

Other Things to Watch For

Height

Take care to check out the height of the space for the refrigerator. As noted in the earlier tables, there is a wide range of heights, even for comparably sized units. If the space is made for a 66¾" high refrigerator then there'll be real problems if someone comes along with a 70½" unit.

Depth

Floor plans for kitchens almost never show the refrigerator much deeper than the adjacent counters. For a 27-cu. ft. unit, the overall depth including the door handles is 36¾", over a foot more than a 24" counter. More modest refrigerators may have depths of over 32 inches, 8" in front of the counter. Sometimes this causes no problems but in others the refrigerator may be in the way or look out of place.

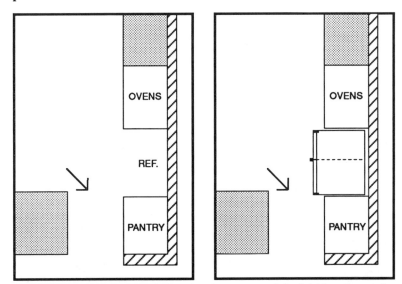

When refrigerators are missing in plans or models, it hides the problems they can cause in passage ways.

Water

Most plumbers use a small recessed metal or plastic box behind the refrigerator in which to terminate the pipe for the refrigerator's ice maker water. This makes the connection more-or-less inside of the wall but, in a Castaic, California tract, the connector for the water is in front of the wall so that the refrigerator must be put several unnecessary inches farther out into the room. Be sure to insist on the recessed arrangement.

Ground-Fault Circuit-Interrupter (GFCI) Protection

Codes require that certain locations in the house be wired with special outlets that prevent you from being fatally shocked if you accidentally touch a water pipe and a hot wire at the same time. TV thrillers to the contrary, you won't be electrocuted if someone throws a hair dryer into the bathtub with you, as long as the dryer is plugged into a bathroom outlet. Bathroom outlets have ground-fault circuit-interrupter protection that instantly turns the power off without harming you. You'll find these special outlets in bathrooms, the kitchen, garage, and outside the house. Even if the actual protection device itself is not present on each outlet, the National Electrical Code requires that all of the outlets in those locations be tied to a GFCI-circuit someplace in the house.

Outlets in which the GFCI unit is an integral part of the outlet are readily identified by having two buttons on them, one marked "TEST" and the other "RESET." If you do something that trips the circuit, you have to push the reset button to get things going again. Manufacturers recommend that you test the circuit monthly by pushing the test button to see if the power goes off, then push the reset button to get back to normal.

A word of warning. The requirements for GFCI are intended for your protection. They are not inclusive. All outlets within six feet of the kitchen sink must have GFCI protection. If your toaster, say, has a short in it and you touch it and the water faucet at the same time, you won't be electrocuted. But if you have a stove top mounted in an island or peninsula, the outlet on the island or peninsula doesn't have to be GFCI protected. Since the stove top is just as grounded as the water faucet, the outlet on the island or peninsula will kill you just as fast as the ones around the sink. If your faulty toaster is plugged in on the island or penin-sula and you touch it and the stove top, it's jolt time!

Don't depend on GFCI protection to keep you out of trouble. Use common sense with appliances and tools. If one has a short or frayed cord, don't use it. You may not have protection where it's plugged in. Don't try to outsmart these things—the life you're endangering is your own.

GFCI outlets cost several times that of a standard outlet. So build-ers and/or the subcontractor try to limit the number they use. They will sometimes run wires all over the place from the outlet with the built-in GFCI circuit to avoid putting in another GFCI outlet.

- In one house we owned there was only one outlet that included the protection circuitry. It was located in the garage and served the entire house. Thus the outlets in both bathrooms, several in the kitchen, and the outlets outside of the house were all tied to this one outlet that had the GFCI circuit. One day I unknowingly tripped the protection circuit from an outside outlet. Because no one had explained all this to me, I spent quite a while before dis-covering why there was no power in the bathroom for my elec-tric razor.

You should expect a GFCI outlet in each room where protection is required. When an outlet is tripped, it can be frustrating and time-consuming to try to find the GFCI protection when it's in a different part of the house.

You'll have at least one outlet with GFCI protection in the garage. If there is more than one outlet, the others may not be protected. The one protected outlet is there for you to use for power tools. The others may be construed as being dedicated for freezers or other large appliances which, according to the National Electrical Code, do not require protection. Similarly, outside of the house you may have a special "T" outlet made to handle only a single plug rather than two. This is probably for a spa. Some building inspectors will let this go by without GFCI protection. If you have one of these, treat it with especial respect. NEVER use an unprotected outlet for the rotisserie motor on your barbecue, electric lawn mower or edger, or outdoor lights.

Labels are available for outlets which say that the outlet is GFCI protected. These are worthwhile. It lets you know to look at the GFCI unit as well as the circuit breaker if power is lost.

Fireplaces

Fireplaces are used for ambience and heating. In today's houses, however, it must be the ambience that's important because, in the energy department, even the wood-burning fireplaces are expensive.

Five different fireplace arrangements were seen during research for the book:

1. Wood burning without a gas lighter.

2. Nominally wood burning with a gas lighter. These were often equipped with gas logs.

3. Top vent (TV) gas fireplaces that vent through the roof.

4. Direct vent (DV) gas fireplaces with short vents to the side of the house.

5. Unvented gas fireplaces.

A problem with any fireplace is its potential for losing heated room air up the flue, whether or not the fireplace is burning. Dampers reduce this potential. When gas is present, there's a concern about using dampers because of the danger that, if the fireplace is not lit, unburned gas could be forced back into the room. (This same danger exists with unvented gas fireplaces.)

When a fire is burning, adequate oxygen must be present in the firebox. When a gas fire is oxygen starved, it can produce carbon monoxide which is, of course, poisonous.

Gas fireplaces that use pilot lights burn this pilot continuously and part of the heat from the pilot is lost up the flue. For this reason the State of California doesn't permit any gas burning appliance or fireplace that uses a "continuously burning pilot light." This energy loss isn't addressed by codes in Washington or Oregon.

Wood-Burning Fireplaces

Some wood burning fireplaces in the Pacific Northwest don't include gas lighters. Whether this is an oversight or a deliberate way to save a few dollars, it's not a user-friendly thing to do. In these houses the home user must start his fires the old-fashioned way, with paper and kindling, adding even more to the inconvenience and messiness of a wood-burning fireplace. Further, the home user doesn't have the option of changing to gas logs if he wants.

Gas Logs

Burning gas logs in a fireplace designed to burn wood is inefficient. Most of the heat goes up the flue. The gas must be turned on manually with a valve located near the fireplace. Gas logs require a match or lighter for starting.

Gas Fireplaces

Fireplaces designed to burn only gas (not gas logs) are far more efficient. When vented, these have claimed efficiencies of 55 percent; when unvented, they recover all the heat from the burning gas. However, unvented fireplaces with no flue have serious drawbacks, as is discussed below.

Gas fireplaces use pilot lights with the attendant minor energy loss. A thermoelectric arrangement makes it possible to turn the fireplace on and off with a wall switch. There is no connection to the house's electricity for this purpose although power is needed when an optional fan is used. During a power outage the house's usual forced air furnace system cannot operate but the gas fireplace can. It can be a source of heat in these kinds of emergencies.

Gas fireplaces are the most commonly-used fireplaces in new homes in the Pacific Northwest. This may seem strange in a part of the country where wood is available virtually for the taking. Gas is already used for heating in most houses and there is no problem in getting it for fireplaces. This and its cleanliness make gas a more attractive choice than wood.

Energy Code Impacts

The regional differences in the kinds of fireplaces are, then, strictly code related. Local energy codes can result in other regional differences. In Livermore, California, for example, wood-burning fireplaces and gas logs are okay but a wood-burning fireplace is not allowed to have a gas lighter. Thus in two adjacent tracts one set of houses has wood burning fireplaces without a gas lighter and the other has gas logs and cannot burn wood.

Except for the Livermore aberration, the usual practice in California is to put gas lighters in wood-burning fireplaces. Thus the home user is given the option, after he moves in, of burning wood or of replacing the gas lighter with gas logs. Not all builders include gas lighters, however.

Combustion Air

The air that all fireplaces need in order to burn is called combustion air. Where this air comes from should be of concern because, except for unvented gas fireplaces, it goes right up the vent pipe. When it comes from inside the building and is then vented outside, the energy that was used to originally heat the air goes out the vent, too.

Gas fireplaces with exhaust flues don't have dampers in them. This results in the loss of heated air up the flue 24-hours a day, whether the fireplace is burning or not. The same thing occurs with wood-burning fireplaces when the damper isn't closed.

- The gas fireplace in my house gets its air through a 4-inch duct under the firebox. The duct could have been connected to get the combustion air from under the house. It wasn't. (Nor, as noted later, would it have made much difference anyway.) To see just how much heated room air might be going out through the fireplace, I put a lighted butane BBQ lighter in front of the duct. (The fireplace was off.) The flame was bent sideways. When the same thing was done when there was a breeze blowing outside, the rush of air into the duct blew out the butane lighter instantly. This is not a way to ascertain how many BTUs the fireplace costs but it demonstrates that this isn't the way to go. It's similar to leaving a 4-inch hole in the ceiling.

1992 Oregon energy codes wouldn't have allowed this. These codes now require that the combustion air duct "shall be capable of

providing all combustion air from the exterior of the dwelling."
(Note the wording "shall be capable of providing" instead of "must
provide.") But will the newer codes prevent this senseless loss of
heat up the flue? Not at all. The firebox appears as if it is sealed.
The glass on the front is gasketed—until you look closely. The
gasketing is on three sides only. Along the bottom of the glass there's
a gap about ¼-inch wide extending all across the front of the firebox. Until there's a requirement that the firebox be sealed and that
all of the combustion air must come from outside the heated house
envelope, there will be no control over the loss of heated air.

- To continue the experiment, the fireplace was lit and the so-called
  combustion-air duct was completely blocked off. The fireplace
  burned just fine. There was more than enough air coming in
  around the glass to keep the fire burning. Even with the duct
  blocked, heated air goes up the flue 24-hours a day. This was veri-
  fied by going to the roof when the fireplace was not burning. The
  exhaust flue was noticeably warmed by the air coming up through
  it.

In some Oregon houses, when it wasn't convenient for the fireplace
installer to get the combustion air from the crawl space, the combustion air duct went to the roof! This duct, which in one house
was at least 25 feet long, was expected to be the source of combustion air. Now, two 4-inch ducts tie the unsealed firebox to the roof,
creating two ways for heated air to rise when the fireplace is off.
This arrangement is even more energy wasteful than having the
combustion air coming from under the house. As a customer-service
representative of the manufacturer put it, he "wouldn't recommend"
such an arrangement.

Washington energy codes don't consider the fireplace combustion
air problem at all.

California energy codes address the heat loss problem by requiring
closeable doors over the entire opening of the firebox. They also
require that the combustion air be taken from outside of the building and that the intake duct have a readily accessible damper. Further, the exhaust flue damper must have a readily accessible control.

All of this sounds good, but it's worthless! First, there are the ex-
ceptions. In California, if the fireplace isn't on an outside wall and
there's a slab floor, the combustion air is allowed by the code to
come from inside the house. But, when gas is piped into the
fireplace, the damper must be blocked open if required by the

manufacturer's installation instructions or the State Mechanical Code. There's nothing that keeps the fireplace user from leaving any flue damper open all the time. In other words, for every fireplace installed under these codes, nothing keeps the flue from being open 24-hours a day. This saves energy? Combine this with no requirement for any kind of a seal on the firebox, other than that it be closeable, and the question rises, "Why bother?" Heat will go up the flue forever. And, unlike an open door or window, the home-user can't do anything about it if he has no flue damper or it's blocked open.

There's at least one type of gas fireplace that does control energy loss even if it does have a continuously burning pilot light: the direct-vent fireplace.

Direct-Vent Gas Fireplace

The direct-vent gas fireplace has a completely sealed firebox. It uses a concentric ducting arrangement—one intake pipe for the combustion air and an outlet duct for the spent exhaust gasses. The duct is short, going directly from the firebox to the outside of the house. It usually requires an outside wall. Two mounting arrangements are commonly used:

1. The front of the fireplace is mounted flush with the inside wall of the room. A chase, on the outside of the house, is built around the back of the fireplace to enclose it. The ducts go through the wall of the chase.

2. The fireplace is placed triangularly across the corner of the room with one side of the triangle being an outside wall.

The manufacturer says these DV fireplaces can also be vented through the roof as long as special concentric ducts are used. Since the units are sealed, this won't result in any loss of heated room air. Inexplicably, this arrangement was not seen in any of the houses visited during research for the book.

There is one word of caution regarding these direct vent fireplaces. Where the vent goes outside it will be very hot. If it's low enough to the ground for children to reach it, some nasty burns could result. The installation should include a way to prevent this from happening.

Unvented Gas Fireplace

The unvented fireplace is a modern-day version of the portable gas heater we had in our house when I was growing up. It burns gas and returns all the combustion products back into the room. In years past many deaths were caused by improperly adjusted gas heaters that generated carbon monoxide. Today's unvented fireplaces include a sensor in the fire box which makes sure there's enough oxygen and turns the fireplace off if there is danger of carbon monoxide.

As discussed in Appendix B, energy codes address the problem of unhealthy air when houses are tightly sealed. The Washington code, in particular, sets up detailed requirements for exchanging the air in the house to keep it fresh. Now along comes the unvented fireplace which dumps both water vapor and carbon dioxide into the house, along with the oxides of any impurities which may be in the gas. It seems incongruous, but these fireplaces are being installed in Pacific Northwest houses. They're cheap and efficient and allowed by codes. Builders aren't engineers and they'll take the least expensive approach. If you care, you may want to be sure you don't get such a fireplace in your home. At least in California, this is no problem. These units use a continuously burning pilot light and are forbidden for that reason.

Insulation Around Fireplaces

One final note. Fireplaces on outside walls should be insulated. Neither the masonry or the metal used in fire boxes is a good insulator. To avoid heat loss through them, the back sides should be enclosed in an insulated chase.

Telephone and Television Wiring

Today there are different ways to wire houses for telephone and television than in the past. For some people, these offer a step forward in convenience. They are described in this appendix.

Telephone

The local telephone company runs a cable from the street to the house for the telephones. The electrical subcontractor wires the house. The interconnection between the house wiring and the telephone company is done in the small plastic interface box found on the side of the house, usually on an outside garage wall.

It used to be that it was normal to have two lines run into houses from the telephone company. Now, because so many people have computer modems and fax machines, many telephone companies have upped this to five lines. More are available if wanted. However, this increased number of lines in the house leads to a different concern—how to wire the house itself.

Old Two-Line Method

The older method is for the electrician to tie all of the telephone jacks together when he is wiring the house. These connections between jacks are done in the walls of the house. It is permanent and is difficult and expensive to change. It is okay for a house with one or two lines where future expansion or changes are not expected.

The Flexible Method

A much more adaptable method is to not tie the telephone lines together in the house but to run the wires from each telephone jack to the telephone interface box where any telephone jack can be connected to any telephone line. The connections can be changed quickly and inexpensively at any time.

The cost for installing this method when the house is being built is more wire, which is not expensive, and using an electrician who knows what he's doing.,

Jack Location

When the house is wired, you should indicate which rooms are to have jacks and, if you and the builder are on top of it, the electrician will be told where the jacks are to go. If he's not told, he'll make his best guess, and this may not coincide with your needs.

In the kitchen, a wall-mounted telephone is often preferable to one that sits on a counter. At least on the wall it won't get in the way.

TV Wiring

Many families have wished they could watch a program on the TV in the family room, while the VCR (also in the family room) plays a tape on a TV set in one of the other rooms. Or they wish both FM sets could be connected to an antenna in the attic or on top of the house.

When the house is wired, the additional cables and outlets to permit this can be included easily. (As with other wiring, once the house is done, it becomes difficult to change.) Sometimes it takes a specialist to look the situation over and estimate what the special wiring costs; other times the electrician can do it. Usually it's as simple as putting in more TV outlets and running multiple cables from each room.

The TV outlets in a house are NOT wired together. Rather, each wall connector has its own cable which is run to a centralized location where the cables are interconnected to the antenna or to the local cable company. This interconnection uses little boxes, called splitters, with three or more cable connectors on them. These units properly split the TV signals to the various TV sets, VCRs, and FM sets.

The interconnection between the cable company and the house cables usually occurs in an area such as the attic where there's protection from the weather. In some locations, however, the interconnections are outside the house. If more than one cable is being run to each outlet location, an interconnection box someplace in the house or garage makes it convenient to change the cable connections to the various outlets as needed.

Indicate which rooms get a TV outlet and, as with the telephone, choose just where the outlets are to go.

Home Builders' Associations

Most builders belong to a local or regional builder's association. This association, in turn, is affiliated with state and national associations. The national association, the National Association of Home Builders (NAHB), is the trade association that represents the home building industry. These associations are for the benefit of the individual members.

The associations, at all levels, represent members before various governmental agencies. They sponsor and work for legislation benefiting the building community. Membership comes from all areas of the building trades. It includes remodelers and small, medium, and large volume builders. Associate memberships include subcontractors, materials dealers, house designers, lenders, and realtors.

Membership in the local association is seen as giving credibility to the member. For the local association, membership is recognized as a sign of professionalism. One local group says it "has a reputation of requiring and maintaining high standards of professionalism."

At the local level the home builders' associations provide group insurance programs, sponsor seminars, and hold periodic meetings and social events. These activities are for the purpose of education, business contacts, and general assistance for the individual member.

On the national level, the NAHB tests and approves new building materials. It has a number of services available to its members that are intended to provide help in a number of areas of home building. It lobbies at all levels of national government to "ensure housing remains a top priority during the formation of national policy." The lobbying activities also involve the individual members who are asked to bring the NAHB message directly to their representatives in Congress. The NAHB has the third-largest trade association Political Action Committee (BUILD-PAC) in the country, raising over $2,000,000 every four years.

It publishes magazines monthly along with other data available to the members upon request. The NAHB sponsors educational seminars and the largest trade show in the country. It is associated with a home warranty program.

NAHB has a Consumer Affairs Department. It "is a source of information on builder-customer service programs." It "monitors the activities of the Federal Trade Commission...and...works to assist builders and consumers in unresolved disputes."

Builders aren't required to belong to the local builder's association. A few don't.

Real Estate People and Their Organizations

Real estate brokers and agents are licensed by the state. They are obligated to obey the state laws. Brokers assume the ultimate responsibility for real estate deals; agents must get the broker's approval before a deal is finalized. It's a means of double checking the legalities involved. Agents work with the seller or buyer in arranging sales or trades of real property, including houses.

A broker is bonded and must have several years experience as an agent before getting his license. The owner of a real estate firm is usually a broker. Large firms will have a number of brokers.

The fee for selling a piece of property or a house is set in an agreement between the selling agent and the seller. The usual arrangement is for no fee to be paid unless and until the property sells. If the buyer's agent is different from the seller's agent then the fees are divided between the two. In most, if not all, states the fee is a matter of negotiation between the seller and his agent. Fees are usually pretty well standardized in an area, although variations of 1 percent are common. Note that these fees are not all profit for anyone. The overheads in terms of advertising, bonding costs, office space, etc., can be significant and must all be paid out of the fees.

In tract developments the buyer doesn't usually have an agent but deals directly with the real estate agent at the model home. This agent may work for a real estate company or directly for the builder. In either case, the fee is included in the sales price for the house. There is no room in the deal for a buyer's agent's fee.

It is not uncommon for both small and large builders to have their own real estate companies for the sale of houses they build. One advantage is that none of the money from the sale of the house goes to an outside real estate company. Another is that it often gets the buyer's old house as a listing to the builder's real estate company.

Before going any further, one thing should be said: "Realtor," "Realtors," and "Realtor-associate" are all registered trademarks of the National Association of Realtors. Only members of that organization are entitled to use these trademarks. Others should be referred to as real estate brokers or real estate agents. Note that, like many other trademarks, the terms are often used in a generic sense, that is, "realtor" instead of real estate agent, etc.

Most real estate brokers and real estate agents belong to a local Board of Realtors. In each state there is a State Association of Realtors and nationally there is the National Association of Realtors. This is a politically powerful organization with over 800,000 members, and is the world's largest trade association.

The national association has a published code of ethics for its members. This code encompasses the relationships between a realtor and his clients and between other realtors.

You'll see the initials GRI after the name of some realtors. Graduate, Realtor Institute is awarded to a realtor after the completion of three one-week courses offered by the state realtor association. This program is for brokers and associates who are involved primarily with single-family homes.

Similarly, CRS indicates that a realtor is a Certified Residential Specialist, having taken extra studies in this particular area.

The local realtors' association usually sponsors a multiple listing system (MLS) in which all properties being sold by the members are put into a computer file accessible to all members who subscribe to the service. It gives the local realtors the ability to sort through the listings and come up with those which most closely meet the needs of a prospective buyer.

Kitchen and Bathroom Exhaust Systems

Exhaust systems, which are used to rid the house of steam, smoke, fumes, and odors, frequently exist because of a code requirement and/or because of a conception on the part of the buying public that they should be there. Unfortunately, too often, in both kitchens and bathrooms, exhaust systems are ineffective in performing the function for which they were intended.

Kitchen Exhaust Systems

Cooktops are almost always equipped with a means for taking smoke, odors, and steam generated at the stove and exhausting it into outside air. Exhaust systems are classified as "downdraft" or "updraft." The fan in the downdraft units sucks the air sideways off the top of the stove and blows it down through a duct that goes outside. An updraft unit uses a fan in a hood which is mounted over the cooktop. It takes the air coming up from the stove and blows it through a duct to an outside vent which is usually on the roof.

Generally speaking, the downdraft units are not as efficient in removing smoke, fumes, etc., as are the updraft units. It's natural for heated air to rise and not to be pulled down or sideways. To try to compensate for this, the fans for downdraft units are typically larger than for updraft.

Exhaust fans are rated by the amount of air they move and by the amount of noise they generate. In model homes you can often look under the hood and see the actual rating in CFM (cubic feet per minute). Typical updraft fans are rated at around 180 to 200 CFM. This appears to be reasonable for daily use. You can get bigger, more expensive, and noisier fans. Downdraft ratings are from 300 to

500 CFM, although at least one manufacturer offers a unit that moves upwards of 1000 CFM. (For comparison, the rating of the fan in a forced air heating system in a 2000 square-foot house is typically about 1350 CFM.)

All these fans are noisy, a very common objection to them. It is the nature of the beast. Generally, the larger the unit, the noisier it is. For this reason downdraft units are generally noisier than updraft units that do the same job. At least one updraft manufacturer puts the fan itself in the attic which, according to the company, makes it quieter. Downdraft systems which have the fan in the duct away from the cooktop to reduce the noise are also available. Both of these arrangements make cleaning the grease off of the fan blades inconvenient.

A note about downdraft units. Pulling the air across the top of the cooktop will lower the temperature of anything cooking on the top. It is more noticeable with larger units than smaller ones.

Some microwave ovens are designed to mount over a cooktop and include an exhaust fan in them. There is no hood. The unit extends only part way over the cooktop and does nothing for the front burners of the stove.

UPDRAFT FANS WILL BE EFFECTIVE ONLY FOR THE STOVE BURNERS WHICH ARE UNDER THE HOOD OR MICROWAVE OVEN. Small hoods for peninsula stoves and the fans in microwave ovens are not going to do a good job. You can see this for yourself if you visit someone who has such a microwave. Boil some water and turn the fan on. When the pot is on a front burner, most of the steam goes into the room but when it is on a back burner, most of the steam will be captured. (And this happens even though a typical microwave oven fan is rated at 230 CFM, which is larger than most updraft units.) Ranges with oven and cooktop in one unit usually have the burners close to the front of the stove, making the associated updraft hood even less effective.

Another way of understanding why hoods are effective for only the burners under them is to consider just how fast a fan makes the air move. We will use for our example a hood which has a 200 CFM fan and is 18" × 30" which almost covers the burners of a cooktop that is 22" deep. The underside of this hood has an area of 3.75 square feet. With the fan full on, the average speed of the air moving across the bottom of the hood is 0.6 miles per hour! This is the gentlest of breezes. So it's not surprising that the hood is effective only for things rising up into it. It does almost nothing for something that doesn't get into the hood on its own, which is why microwave ovens with exhaust fans are not effective for the front burners of the cooktop. Increasing the amount of air the fan moves will obviously help, but twice "almost nothing" still isn't very much.

There are two styles of updraft hoods, one for when the cooktop is against a wall and one for peninsula use. (Island cooktops don't usually have a hood but rather use downdraft exhaust units.) When there is no back wall to block stray air movement, the area of a peninsula hood is made larger to increase the likelihood that fumes from the cooktop will be captured by the hood. The larger hood takes a bigger fan to get the same air speed at the bottom of the hood.

- It was enlightening to actually watch an exhaust fan do its job when barbecuing on an island grill with a downdraft fan. When the air in the room was quiet, the fan got rid of most of the smoke, but not all. However, there was a ceiling fan about 12 feet away in the kitchen nook and, when this fan was on, the effectiveness of the downdraft fan was clearly very poor.

  A similar experiment was carried out with an updraft fan over a peninsula cooktop. The hood apparently protected the cooktop to a large extent from the ceiling fan. There wasn't a noticeable difference when the ceiling fan was on or off.

- Downdraft fans will be even less effective in venting steam from a tall pot of boiling water, such as is used to cook pasta. Downdraft units that run a piece of metal up behind the cooktop when the fan is on may help, but the ability of the fan to pull steam and smoke sideways from the space over the cooktop will require a significantly larger fan than an updraft hood. Even then, it simply cannot be as effective.

For best operation there shouldn't be other air movement around the cooktop, particularly with a downdraft unit. When there's a ceiling fan in the neighborhood, downdraft units won't do as well as cooktops that have the protection of hoods. Updraft units against a wall, where there's even more protection, will suffer least from air movement from open windows or doors, house heating or cooling systems, and ceiling fans.

Ductless Exhaust

"Ductless," "recirculating," "no vent," or "no duct" is a nice way of saying that whatever the fan picks up from the stove will be passed through a charcoal filter and dumped back into the room. When it's not vented outside, the exhaust system does very little good. It filters the heated air, smoke, fumes, and steam coming up from the stove and will take out some of the larger particles in the smoke. It cannot, however, trap most of the smoke or fumes and none of the water vapor or hot air that's sucked up by the fan. In short, it is about as close to useless as you'd want to have. A magazine article rated this arrangement as "5% effective." The Washington State Ventilation and Indoor Air Quality Code doesn't allow them, requiring that "All ducts shall terminate outside the building."

The usual place where you'll see a ductless or re-circulating exhaust system is in a microwave oven. But, microwave ovens aren't the only place where a ductless system can be found. National manufacturers of kitchen exhaust systems make updraft units that aren't a part of a microwave oven but which can be used in a ductless mode.

• Finding these ductless systems is easy. If the power is on, simply turn the fan on and see if the air comes back into the room from the louvered area at the top of the microwave or hood. If it does, you're looking at a ductless exhaust. If the power isn't on, open up the cupboard above the microwave to see if there's duct work there. If there is, fine. If not, you've probably got a ductless exhaust, although it's possible to vent the exhaust directly through the back wall without any duct work showing in the cabinet above the unit. If you really want to know, check it with the power turned on.

Ductless systems are also available for downdraft units. They won't be effective there, either.

One of the most annoying things about these systems, aside from their uselessness, is that they blow the air back into the room at just about head height. Having a blast of whatever is coming from the stove blowing in your face is not very friendly.

• One woman reported that she had a microwave oven with a ductless exhaust fan installed when she remodeled her house. With the combination of air blowing in her face and the overall uselessness of the unit, she opens a window next to the stove when she needs to have smoke exhausted. Most of us don't have windows close to the cooktop, nor do we feel like pouring money down a rat hole to get a useless piece of machinery.

Manufacturers don't recommend the use of ductless units if there is any way to duct them outside. But, as one customer representative said on the telephone, "They're better than nothing." Well, maybe. They're used in new houses in California and Oregon, not because there's no other choice, but so the builder can save a few dollars. They add glitz by paying attention to customer's expectations but there's no substance. They get into new houses for one or both of two reasons:

1. The builder doesn't know better.

2. The builder is trying to save a few bucks on the duct work.

In either case, the use of these ductless arrangements is about as user-unfriendly as you get.

Other Stove and Exhaust System Considerations

The height of an exhaust system above the cooktop is important. The lower the exhaust system, the better. But too low will put the hood or microwave oven in the way for cooking. Too high will make the exhaust system even more sensitive to extraneous air movement. A suggested compromise is 21" for microwave ovens and 24" for hoods that stick out in front.

Note that 24" would put the bottom of a microwave oven just five feet above the floor, making it difficult for a short person to see what's happening in the oven.

A common complaint about exhaust hoods is the appearance. There are two designs that address this. Both use movable parts that are brought into use only when needed. One is a simple flap that is pulled out from the front of the hood to try to increase the effective size of the hood.

In the other design, the part that pulls out is much more than just a flap. It is the full height of the hood and includes a part of the exhaust system filter. When it is not in use, the movable part is back even with the front of the adjoining cabinets. The front of the hood may be glass, black or white enamel to match the stove, or the same wood used in the cabinets. The unappealing appearance associated with hoods is gone.

The entire under surface of the hood is covered with filters. Lights, which are an integral part of the hoods, are above the filters so that they must shine through to illuminate the stove top.

The manufacturer (Imperial Cal, Irvine, California) offers these in versions with 300 and 400 CFM, both of which are significantly larger (and noisier) than most updraft exhaust systems.

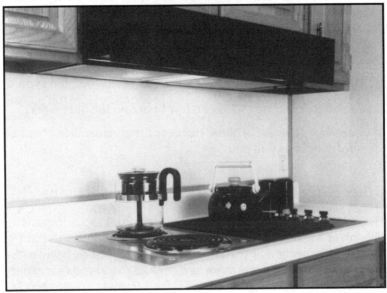

Pullout updraft exhaust system manufactured by Imperial Cal.

Bathroom and Laundry Exhaust Systems

Codes allow ventilation in bath and laundry rooms to be accomplished either using a window or an exhaust fan. Most of today's homes include an exhaust fan. This is a good idea even if there's a window present because in the winter you'd probably rather use the exhaust fan than open a window.

Unfortunately, most bathroom and laundry exhaust fans pay lip-service to the code but don't do much for ventilation. To meet the code a fan with a capacity of 60 cubic feet per minute (CFM) will usually do the trick. The cost of such a fan is around $20 for the subcontractor. In a typical installation, a 4" flexible aluminum duct is tied to the fan to take the exhausted air outside the house as is required by the building codes. At the lower end of the duct is a flap that keeps cold air from coming down the duct when the fan isn't operating. The fan must push air hard enough to open the flap then get the air up 10 , 20 or more feet of duct. The $20 fan can't do this. So we have a situation where builders put in the fan with a rating of 60 CFM when there's no back pressure on it and then put it in a situation where it can't work. Most building inspectors know this but have bigger problems to worry about. So you get a useless exhaust fan. (Try turning these fans on and then go up on the roof and see what comes out. If you have one of these $20 jobs, it won't be much.)

A part of the reason that nobody seems to care whether a fan does its job or not is that there's a real question of just how necessary a fan is in the first place. If you want it to get smells out, then you'd better get one that'll deliver the 60 CFM (or more) when it's actually installed, not when it's sitting in a test lab by itself. If it's moisture you're trying to get rid of, you may ask yourself just how important that is in today's houses. If you want to give an impression that something is really happening then go along with the $20 fan; they make enough noise to make everyone think they must be doing a great job!

Another place where fans are ineffective, in fact just plain useless, is in a modern open bath/shower that's an extension of the bedroom. Here the area to vent is much larger. Fans meet the letter of the code. They can't possibly do anything else. Should the codes be changed? Probably.

Cabinets

In today's houses the cabinetmaker does both the kitchen and bathroom cabinets. Not surprisingly they usually look much alike, both inside and out. In this appendix, cabinets for both locations are discussed without distinctions between them.

Perceptions About Cabinets

Fads in cabinets are continually changing, both nationally and locally. The in thing right now is the use of hidden hinges that are invisible from the front of the cabinets. There are significant drawbacks to the use of these hinges. Cabinetmakers prefer them because they allow simpler adjustments for cabinet doors than are possible with the older types of hinges. As long as they're popular with the public and are favored by the cabinetmakers, we can expect to see them around for a while. Their disadvantages are discussed later.

Choices of both hinges and cabinet material involve perceptions on the part of the individual. The following discussions attempt to present the pros and cons independent of current or regional preferences of the moment.

Cabinet Exteriors

Cabinet exteriors offer many choices. The first decision is whether to use a wood (natural) finish or to paint them. If a wood finish is chosen, you need to choose the type of wood. Whether painted or stained, the finish color will be need to be selected. Generally, cabinets throughout the house are given the same finish but it is not a requirement.

Cabinet exteriors range from plain to decorative. You may prefer finger grooves to open the doors or choose from a variety of hardware pulls. Should the cabinets go all the way to the ceiling? If not, should the space above them (the soffits) be boxed in? If you are making the decision about boxing in the soffits, don't forget the vent for the exhaust fan. If the exhaust system is an updraft unit, it will need a duct going up through the ceiling. The duct work will need to be covered up, either by boxing it in or hiding it with tall cabinets.

When the soffits are boxed in, differently colored paint or wall paper is sometimes used on the wallboard above the cabinets to add a decorative or festive touch to the kitchen.

Tall Cabinet Doors

Here's a word of caution about very tall cabinets: wood warps. Cabinet doors are no exception and, when they're warped, they are apt to rattle or bang when you close them. Tall doors are more likely to do this than shorter ones. This problem was seen in many tracts in California and in houses in a recent Portland, Oregon "Street of Dreams."

Some cabinet manufacturers add stiffeners to the inside of tall cabinet doors. These will reduce warping but not twisting of the doors. In southern California some tall cabinet doors have catches on them to overcome the effects of warping. These make the opening of the doors more difficult and add one more piece of hardware that can malfunction. Tall doors are, more often than not, unsatisfactory.

Another consideration with cabinets that go to the ceiling is that the top shelves are useful only for storing things you almost never need, because you have to use a chair or a ladder to get to them.

Cabinet Interiors

Melamine

Plastic laminate (melamine) has become popular for the insides of cabinets and drawers because of its resistance to wear and its ease of cleaning. The basic plastic is the same material as is used in laminate (Formica) countertops. It is usually laminated directly onto particle board. Some cabinetmakers will paint shelf edges which doesn't do a particularly good job of covering the particle board. Others use a pre-fabricated vinyl strip that's attached to the shelf.

Usually this plastic is white but colors and even patterns are available. White has a hospital-like appearance which is displeasing to some people. Besides the tough, easy-to-clean aspects of plastic laminate, it is popular with cabinet makers because it is cheaper and it doesn't have to be finished as wood does.

The edges of melamine-clad shelves and interiors should be smooth and clean. In cheap cabinets seen in many places in California, the edges look like they had been cut with a hatchet.

Wood

Finished wood is found in better cabinets and drawer interiors. Good finishes on interior wood surfaces can be quite durable while poor finishes will stain, become dirty, and be difficult to keep clean. Well made and finished wooden interiors will always have a richness in appearance that's not possible with plastic.

Particle Board

Particle board is used in cheap cabinets. If the cabinets are not to be painted, two options are available: 1) a wood grain is printed on the surface or 2) a thin layer of wood is laminated to it. For painted cabinets this isn't necessary and the paint is applied directly to the particle board. Most people cover particle board shelves with a thin plastic lining or even vinyl linoleum to give a surface which can be easily cleaned and maintained. With better-quality cabinets this isn't necessary.

Backs

How the backs of cabinets are handled speaks loads about their quality. Cheap cabinets won't have a back. They'll have 1" × 2" or 1" × 3" boards (nailing strips) for screwing to the wall and that's all. The underlying wallboard is exposed and the whole arrangement looks cheap. Better cabinets will have be backed with the same material as the rest of the interior; wood, or melamine. Look for the joints where the cabinet back and the sides meet. In well-made cabinets this joint will be smooth and tight. Sloppily made cabinets will show definite, unattractive gaps.

Mountings

The nailing strip used to hang cabinets from a back wall is typically made from wood, plywood, or melamine-coated particle board. In good cabinets the material will have the same surface as the cabinet back and walls so that it matches the rest of the cabinet interior. Particularly for the melamine-coated particle board, this may result in a visible unfinished edge on the nailing strip which should be covered or painted to match the melamine but sometimes is not. Mounting screws used in better cabinets are not visible but are covered by special plastic buttons. (These are inexpensive and easy to use. Good cabinetmakers put them in place when the cabinets are installed. The who-cares installers don't bother. Actually it's something you can do yourself but you shouldn't have to.)

Cabinet Styles

There are two distinctly different cabinet styles; western or face-frame and European or box. In western-style cabinets the front edges of the sides of the cabinet are covered by a ring of wood, the face frame. This ring is missing in European-style cabinets so that the cabinet looks like a box from the front.

In a western-style cabinet the face frame is clearly visible around the edges of closed doors, at least on the top and sides of the cabinet. When two cupboards are adjacent, a common face frame piece is used. The width of the face frame varies from one cabinet to another, depending upon the design and manufacturer.

With western-style cabinets, traditional hinge units are visible from the front of the cabinet along the edges of the doors. These hinges are made of thin pieces of metal that mount to the door and to the side of the face frame. Doors open a full 180 degrees and, when open, the cabinet opening is obstructed only by the face frame and the thin metal of the hinge mounting.

The space behind the face frame is useful for storage when shelves don't pull-out. With pull-out shelves, however, this space is lost because shelves must be narrower than the inside of the face frame.

Cabinet Hinges

With box (European-style) cabinets, which have no face frame, closed doors cover the front edges of the cabinet sides. When two cupboards are adjacent, their sides and doors are right next to each other. With this proximity the doors must be adjusted carefully both for proper operation and for appearance. This is accomplished by using a style of hinge that mounts on the inside of the cabinet wall and which is easily adjustable in the sideways, in-out, and the up-down directions. This is the European-style hinge.

The European-Style Hinge

In the European-style hinge the door part of the hinge fits into a 3.5 cm. (1⅜") diameter round shallow hole cut into the back of the door. The cabinet part of the hinge is typically about ½" wide, ½" to ¾" thick, and 2" long. The long part of the hinge has mounting feet for the screws that mount it to the inside of the cabinet.

The hinge pin itself is inside the door, i.e., is inside of the hole cut into the door. As a result of this construction:

1. Doors don't open much past straight out, and

2. When open, the inside edge of an open door doesn't clear the cabinet opening thus reducing the effective size of the opening.

Having the door hinge this way is necessary so that adjacent doors on a cabinet don't hit each other (remember that, without a face frame, doors on adjacent cupboards are themselves adjacent.)

These hinges, while invisible from the front of the cabinet when the doors are closed, are large and very visible when the doors are open.

The European-style hinge is mounted on the inside of the cabinet wall, reducing the clear width of the cabinet. This, plus the fact that open doors don't clear the opening, means that pull-out shelves in European-style cabinets have the same problem as in face-frame cabinets—the useful shelf width is noticeably less than the inside width of the cabinet.

Hidden Hinges with Face-Frame Cabinets

The perception that a hidden hinge is *the* thing to have and the popularity with cabinet makers have conspired to cause a bastardization of the European-style hinge for use with face-frame cabinets. The mounting feet for the hinge are simply moved forward so that they mount on the inside of the face frame rather than on the inside walls of the cabinet.

This is a lousy design for two reasons:

1. The useful front opening of the cabinet is reduced in width by both the face frame and the thickness of the hinges.

2. The long side of the European-style hinge juts back behind the face frame leaving an unsightly and useless gap between it and the inside wall of the cabinet.

The result of 1) is that pull-out shelves must be even narrower. The problem with 2) is that the unattractiveness of the European-style hinge is accentuated even further. The only good thing that you can say about the arrangement is that cabinetmakers can do a sloppier job with the doors and still use them because of the adjustment capability which is an integral part of the hinge.

What's really irritating about this misuse of the hinge is that there's a design that's hidden and is specifically intended for use with face-frame cabinets. This is a compact hinge which uses some of the design ideas of the European-style hinge but mounts to the face frame with a flat plate similar to the traditional face-frame hinge. Simple adjustments move the door up-down and sideways. Unlike the bastardized European-style hinge, an open door is moved clear of the cabinet opening in normal face-frame fashion.

Misuse of the European-style hinge occurs with custom cabinetmakers, while pre-manufactured cabinet makers use the more appropriate compact hinge.

There is a serious drawback to all of these hidden hinges, whether used in box or face-frame cabinets; they do not open much past straight out. Even a cursory examination shows that, when they are open as far as they'll go, there's so much leverage at the outside edge of the door that a small child could ruin a door or cabinet by pushing it. For cabinets above a kitchen counter this isn't a severe problem, but for base cabinets it is always a danger, particularly with a growing family.

When you're deciding about cabinets, remember that "new" and "in" aren't necessarily better. The older face frame cabinets and their visible hinges may well be the best for you. It appears that a cabinet with a minimum-width face frame would be optimal in terms of minimizing the space loss when used with pull-out shelves.

Center Mullions

Some cabinet designs have a piece of wood, called a center mullion, mounted vertically up the center of the front opening. The cabinet doors close against this mullion. This design is deadly to the use of pull-out shelves because it means you end up with two much smaller shelves. The mullions are in the way even without pull outs. Except in very wide cabinets, center mullions are used for cosmetic, not practical, reasons. If you're planning on pull-out shelves either initially or you plan to change over to them at some future time, DO NOT choose a cabinet design with a center mullion.

Pull-Out Shelves

In pantries and in other cabinets, shelves may be adjustable up and down, they may be pull-out, or they may be fixed in place. When shelves are deep, typically 22" to 24", articles in the back of them are difficult to reach. For these cases, pull-out shelves make a lot of sense.

- But there's more to it than just having pull-out shelves. One builder's houses in Tacoma, Washington have pull-out shelves all right. Below the counter, a cabinet about 30 inches wide with a shelf has a pair of double doors on the front. Instead of having the doors simply meet at the center of the cabinet, there is a center mullion some two or three inches wide. The doors close over this. Even without being pull-out, the shelf's usefulness would be severely limited by the mullion.

   But there are two sets of pull-out shelves in the cabinet, one set behind each door! With the space lost for the two sets of pull-out hardware plus the space taken by the center mullion in front, close to half of the space that should have been available for storage is lost.

The amount of storage space is reduced when shelves are made pull-out because of the room taken by the slide hardware. However, the increased accessibility to the back of deep shelves will usually more than make up for the reduction in shelf width.

Beware of pull-out shelves in which the front of the pull-out shelf hardware is not covered. Regardless of how careful you are, sooner or later someone will pull out a shelf without fully opening the cabinet doors. If the front of the pull-out sliders is left uncovered, this will result in gouging the interior finish of the partly-opened door. Some cabinetmakers put a piece of plastic in front of the slide hardware so that the plastic hits the door first, virtually eliminating the problem. The usual arrangement has the front of the shelf extending out to cover the hardware. But beware that some custom cabinetmakers aren't up to speed on these things.

The simplest pull-out design is just the shelf with slides mounted on each side. These have no sides or backs. Then there are those with fronts, sides, and backs several inches high, looking more like a parts bin in a hardware store than a shelf. These are sometimes called trays. Unless someone is expected to slam these shelves around and try to knock things off of them, there seems little reason for other than minimal front, side and back pieces, if any at all. Such pieces take away from the space available for storage as well as add to the cost. But, again here, personal preference should be the determining factor. If you have a choice, get what satisfies you.

While pull-out shelves can usually be added to an existing cabinet, this is not always the case. In models in Agoura and Tracy, California, the cabinets are irregularly shaped, making pull-out shelves impossible. These are both deep cupboards so that the home users are forever saddled with a large amount of virtually unusable cabinet spaces.

Pull-out shelves can make the bottom of vanity cabinets much more useful. Unfortunately, it is only rarely that builders and cabinet-makers pay any attention to this need. Give it serious consideration in your new home.

Lazy Susans

In corners of kitchen cabinets there will often be locations where fixed shelves leave areas which are almost inaccessible. In these cases a lazy-Susan type of arrangement is usually appropriate. These are more expensive than fixed shelves but end up providing more useful shelf space. These are available for below-the-counter cabinets in a number of different styles. Lazy Susans can also be used in the upper cabinets in kitchens although they're not as popular because the shelves aren't as deep.

Drawer Boxes

The sides of drawer boxes may be connected to the fronts and backs in two different ways. In one, the pieces are dove-tailed, i.e., they are cut and grooved so that they intermesh at the corners. In the other, the pieces are simply butted and then stapled, nailed or screwed. In all cases the pieces are glued. Dove-tailing is "better" in that it has a more hand-crafted look and is more expensive. Because of the glue, both approaches are more than sturdy enough for cabinet drawers. In a very expensive house, expect dove-tailed drawer boxes; in starter homes expect stapled pieces. It's a matter of cost and taste. Utility doesn't enter into it. (Dove tailing is used only with wood, not with melamine or particle board.)

Recycling Bins

A new trend in cabinetry for today's environmentally conscious society is to have built-in recycling bins for used bottles and cans. They are a convenient amenity if you have room.

• In one house near Portland, Oregon, the home buyer carried this to the extreme and does not have a disposal in the sink. What isn't recyclable has its own bin and this is carried to the garbage can. For her sake let's hope that when she gets ready to sell her house she can find a buyer who is as enthusiastic about not having a disposal as she is. Getting power under the sink and a switch on the wall isn't that easy after the house has been completed.

Custom vs. Pre-manufactured Cabinets

Cabinets may be either pre-manufactured units from a large manufacturer or custom made from a smaller, usually local, shop. Custom cabinets are generally more expensive and are usually thought to be of better quality than pre-manufactured units. This may or may not be the case. Actually you pretty much get what you pay for in both custom and pre-manufactured cabinets. Cheap is cheap regardless of who makes them.

Local custom cabinetmakers often don't finish the cabinets in their shops. This is done on site after the cabinets are installed. Generally speaking, the conditions for finishing the cabinets on the site are far from ideal. Temperature is not controlled nor is the amount of dust in the air. A principal reason that the small cabinet makers don't finish their cabinets in their shops is that they can't! There are stringent OSHA and environmental protection rules that have to be obeyed and it's expensive to equip a shop to do finishing. In a house under construction, this is not required.

The quality of finishing should be about the same regardless of where it is done—if it's done properly. Since there's less likelihood of getting a proper job on the site than in a shop, it's fair to assume that pre-finished cabinets are the better choice if you have an option. (This same logic suggests that advertising which says that "site finished cabinets" are preferable is misleading.)

It is important that the cabinets are installed properly. You have a right to expect this for both custom-made and pre-manufactured units. This also applies to the design of the custom-made cabinets and to the choice of the correct units for pre-manufactured ones.

One of the more annoying things seen in kitchens with microwave ovens is that the doors on the cabinets just above the ovens come down too far. When knobs or handles are used, this is no problem. When the design uses finger grooves and the doors are too close to the oven it is annoyingly difficult to get the doors open. The cabinet design should take into account that the top of the microwave oven typically sticks out in front of the cabinet doors so that there must be enough space between door and oven to comfortably insert one's fingers.

Cabinet Bases

Counter heights for kitchens are pretty standard at around 36". Some islands with stove tops are higher. In bathrooms which may be used by children, it's common to put the counters lower, typically 32". In the master bedroom vanity area, however, there are a variety of heights, the argument being that the higher counters are more comfortable for an adult and there's no reason to make them low enough for children. You may want to give this some thought.

Watch out for custom cabinets in which the base, the part of the cabinet that sits on the floor, isn't mitered at the corners. This is generally ¾" plywood with a hardwood surface. From the front of the cabinet the unmitered corners look fine but, if the cabinet is where it can be seen from the end, the view is of the edge of a piece of plywood, not the hardwood surface. Fortunately this unusually sloppy piece of work isn't common but it does happen.

Rounded Corners

In kitchens there may be a number of outside cabinet corners both above and below the counter. Some manufacturers will make these rounded rather than square. It's a cosmetic consideration; if this idea appeals to you, check out their availability and cost.

Design Information

If you decide to buy a copy of an existing set of cabinets then most of the following decisions are already made, otherwise you'll have to make the following choices for your new cabinets:

1. Kind of wood.

2. Face fame or European style?

3. Door pattern.

4. Exterior finish.

5. Interior finish. (Be sure that the cabinets have backs, that all of the nailing strip is finished like the rest of the interior and that screw heads are covered.)

6. Shelf finish. (If melamine, be sure that the front edges of shelves are properly finished and that cut edges are clean, i.e., not chipped.)

7. Use finger grooves, knobs, or pulls. Where are they to be placed?

8. Where to have shelves and where to put drawers in below-the-counter cabinets.

9. Are the shelves adjustable up and down? How?

10. Are below-the-counter shelves to be pull out? What kinds of fronts and sides do you want on pull-out shelves?

11. Kinds of hinges.

12. Finish on the inside of drawers.

13. Are drawer boxes to be dovetailed?

14. Built-in cutting board?

15. One or more narrow vertical cupboards for storing cookie sheets, cutting boards, and the like?

16. Are external corners to be rounded?

17. In internal corners, is there to be a lazy Susan below the counter? How about above the counter?

18. Do you want the little tip-out storage units under the sink?

Countertops

The basic materials used for countertops are laminates (popularly known by the trade name Formica), ceramic tile, cultured marble, and solid surface. Cultured marble and solid surface countertops are both cast polymers, but of different materials.

There are significant regional differences in the materials used in countertops. For example, in Arizona and California, bathroom vanity tops may be ceramic tile but are usually cultured marble. At the same time, in the Pacific Northwest laminate is the most common, while tile is used to a certain extent in move-up and more expensive homes. Cultured marble is rarely seen.

Ceramic tile is popular in new California kitchens except in some of the more luxurious homes where you'll find more expensive solid-surface counters (Corian, et al). Laminate is found only at the very bottom of the price range. In the Pacific Northwest, laminates are used extensively in kitchens even in more expensive homes.

In many places (California, for one), kitchen counters usually have the sink either mounted flush with the counter or mounted below the level of the tile. This, of course, makes cleaning the counters much easier than when there is a lip or rim in the way. In the Pacific Northwest, on the other hand, the sinks are virtually always dropped into the counters from above, leaving the lip above the countertop, a most unsatisfactory arrangement for cleaning. In keeping with the growing popularity of no-lip countertops, at least one company (Kohler) is expanding its line of "tile-in" and "undercounter" kitchen sinks. The tile-in unit is made with square corners to be mounted flush in a tile counter and the undercounter sink is made with wide rims for use under tile or solid surface counters.

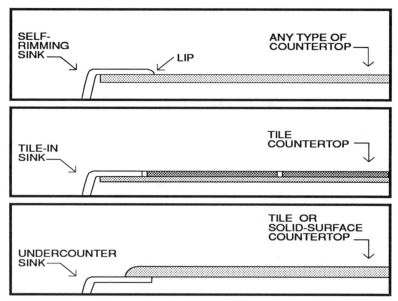

Self-rimming or drop-in sinks have get-in-the-way lips on top of the counter. The others do not.

Each material has its advantages and disadvantages. The following discussion compares their characteristics.

Wood and the more exotic materials like stone (marble, granite) are not discussed because they were seen infrequently in countertops in today's new homes.

The items of concern for countertops are:

• Appearance.

• Cost.

• Resistance to day-to-day wear. More a concern in kitchens than elsewhere.

• Resistance to cutting or scratching. Again a kitchen concern.

• Hardness. A hard surface resists cutting, scratching and wear. It will crack or chip if mistreated. Hard surfaces are more likely to cause breakage to glass or china objects dropped on them.

- Sink mounting. Can sinks or basins be mounted flat with or below the counter surface, thus permitting debris to be wiped directly into the sink?

- Day-to-day maintenance.

- Repairability.

Laminates

The least expensive countertops are the laminates. These are made of a thin, hard, tough plastic sheet which is glued (laminated) to a piece of backing material for strength. Laminates are not as hard as other materials. This is a disadvantage in that they are easier to cut with a knife, but an advantage because dishes or glasses dropped on a laminate counter are not as likely to break.

Sinks and basins used with laminates are top mounted through a hole cut in the material. The sinks have a lip that sits on top of the counter. Sinks are available with a stainless steel rim that is relatively thin which makes it easier to wipe the counter. An objection to sinks with the stainless steel rim is that dirt tends to build up along the edge of the rim giving it a small, but noticeable, dark, unclean appearance.

Laminates are relatively easy to clean but, if scratched, they will hold dirt. Because of their softness, be careful about cutting or burning them. Scorches cannot be repaired except by replacing a section of the counter.

Seams in laminates are usually obvious.

Laminates come in many colors with and without patterns. There are two fundamental ways to make backsplashes and counter fronts:

- The countertop, the backsplash, and the counter front are formed from a single piece of material. There is a raised lip at the front edge of the countertop.

- Only flat pieces are used with the backsplash being a separate piece. The front edge is also a separate piece of laminate.

Improperly manufactured laminate counters may separate from their underlying material making a lump in the surface. This should not occur but does occasionally.

One-Piece Countertops

From the user's point of view, having the backsplash and the lip molded as a single piece has two distinct advantages: 1) There is no joint where the top meets the backsplash nor where it meets the front piece, and 2) the front lip helps keep water from dripping on the floor.

There is a disadvantage, also. At inside corners, with a 2-foot deep counter, there will be a 45-degree seam which is about 34 inches long going from the corner at the front of the counter to the back corner of the backsplash. Laminate seams are never things of beauty and some people object to the appearance of this long seam. Further, it takes special machinery to do a precise job of making the seam and not all countertop manufacturers have it. It's a tricky business, at best.

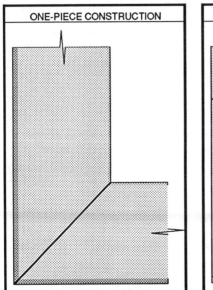
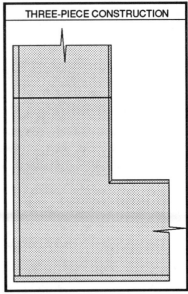

ONE-PIECE CONSTRUCTION   THREE-PIECE CONSTRUCTION

With one-piece laminate countertops, long seams are necessary at corners. With three-piece countertops the seams are less obvious.

Three-piece Countertops

The inside corner problem can be avoided when the countertop is made with flat pieces of laminate. By cutting the corner section out of a single sheet of the laminate, seams, if any are needed at all, occur in a straight line from front to back of the counter. Virtually anyone can make counters in this way, leading to a wide variety of designs. Sometimes tile is used for the backsplash to add a little variety. Other times wood is used for the same purpose. Counter fronts may also be laminate or may be wood. To break the monotony, front edges may be beveled and faced with either the laminate or with wood. The variations seem to be limited only by the imaginations of the counter makers.

Ceramic Tile

Ceramic tiles come in many sizes, shapes, colors and grades. Only vitreous ceramic tile should be used for kitchen and bathroom counters. These are harder, stronger, and more resistant to water absorption than are the lesser grades of tile.

Tiles are glued to the underlying material with spaces between tiles. These spaces are then filled with grout. When grout is set or hardened, any bending of the underlayment will cause the grout to crack. (When used on floors a rigid underlayment must be used.)

Tiles are resistant to knife cuts (the usual result will be to dull the knife) but it's possible to scratch the hard surface. This can be repaired by replacing the tile. Be sure to have a small supply of every tile piece you have in your house so that it can be replaced if needed. Also keep a record of the manufacturer and color of the grout. Thoughtful tile installers will leave a piece or two of each tile shape.

Tile surfaces are harder than cultured marble or solid surface materials. They have virtually no give so that a glass or a dish dropped on them will break easier than with other counters.

Tile counters lend themselves to mounting the kitchen sink either level with the countertop or below it. When recessed, the sink may be stainless steel or cast iron.

Matching Tiles

Did you ever notice tile installations where the tile pieces along the edges are a different length than the rest so that there are two sets of grout lines, one for the edges and a different one for the rest of the counter? This doesn't have to be. It's just uncaring, sloppy work.

Counters usually use the same tile for the backsplash. Rounded pieces of tile (called "bullnose") are then used to give a finished look to the top row of tile. Tiles come in many different sizes, with

4¼" and 6" square tiles being common. If you have a backsplash with 4¼" tiles, it is common for the installer to finish it off with 6" rounded trim pieces. This is what causes two sets of grout lines.

This has been done so commonly that some people have become used to it and don't object to the appearance. However, many people find this very amateurish. If trim pieces are available the same size as the tile, then they should be used so that the grout lines line up in a neat and orderly fashion.

- In one unfinished house in Tigard, Oregon, an installer was putting tile in a tub surround and the edge pieces weren't lining up with the tile. In this case the tile was 6" × 8" and the edge pieces were 6" long. However, the way the tile was laid, the 6" edge pieces were finishing the 8" side of the tile! When the installer was asked if he didn't think it made a nicer looking job with the grout lines lined up, he said that, no, he liked the random appearance of the two sets of grout lines. He'd probably like a polka-dot house, too.

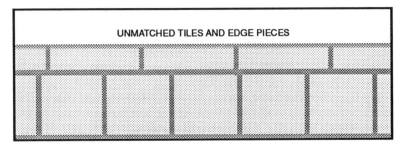

UNMATCHED TILES AND EDGE PIECES

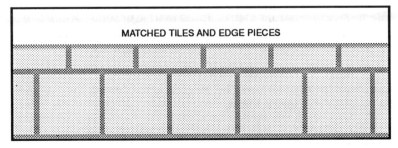

MATCHED TILES AND EDGE PIECES

Properly chosen and installed tile and edge pieces look like they belong together.

To each his own, but if you want your tile job to look like the tile and the edge pieces came from the same place, it is suggested that you make this desire known to the builder and the tile installer. Be sure, too, that tiles and trim pieces of the same size are available in the tile pattern you select. It's a good investment in time to have it done right.

Decorative Effects

Sometimes the backsplash will use a special decorative tile with a pattern in it to give a more appealing look to the counter, particularly in bathrooms. Patterns can be made with ceramic tile by simply cutting the tiles in halves, for example, and installing them at angles to give a different-looking surface. This ability to have patterns in individual tiles as well as in the overall tiled surface is one of the attractions of tile, particularly for large surfaces such as shower stalls and tub surrounds.

Maintenance

Tile can present a maintenance problem. While good tiles themselves are impervious to just about anything, the grout is not and a special sealer is often needed to protect it from staining. This is a problem on kitchen counters where there are many things that can cause stains. It is also a problem in baths where showers may not be wiped down after each use. Over a period of time deposits can build up on the tile and grout, particularly when the water is hard. This is not always easy to remove.

Tile won't burn. Care should be exercised, however, about putting something very hot on it because tile can crack from thermal stress.

In selecting a grout color, particularly for kitchens, note that light colored grouts are more likely to show stains and discoloration than are darker ones. Your supplier should tell you this, but it's sometimes overlooked. If you can, choose a darker grout color because it's easier to maintain.

For many years a concern about tile was that the mildew could grow in the grout. Its surface is relatively porous and it will hold water, a problem that is more pronounced in damp climates. When microscopic nutrients that sustain mildew growth get mixed with this water, then mildew occurs. Today, however, new houses are considerably drier than older ones and grouts include chemicals to inhibit mildew growth, so there's no longer the same concern.

Workmanship

Good and bad workmanship in tile installations is usually obvious; tiles don't lay flat, grout lines aren't straight, etc. Proper edge-cutting is another indication of the quality of the work. Inevitably there will be places where the installer will have to cut a piece of tile or trim to make it fit the available space. These cuts, whether made with a saw or made by scribing the tile and snapping (breaking) it will leave edges which are sharp and, sometimes, rough. A tile-cutting saw makes cleaner cuts than does a snap cutter.

These edges can be smoothed and rounded by using fine sandpaper or a grind stone. The color of a piece of tile is in the surface material which is a glaze on the main body of the tile. When the glaze and the body are distinctly different colors, as they sometimes are, then rounding the edges too much lets the underlying color show through. This should never be a problem if a saw is used to cut the tile. Rounding should only be necessary to smooth the sharp edge and not to smooth away a lot of chips.

Cultured Marble

'Cultured marble' is not what its name implies. It isn't cultured and it isn't marble although the finished material can have a marble-like appearance. It is made with limestone, the same mineral as natural marble.

The Mix

Cultured marble is manufactured by mixing finely ground limestone with a polyester resin which is poured into a mold and allowed to set. Cultured marble is made in solid colors and with colors which swirl through it, simulating the appearance of natural marble. Colors are mixed in the limestone-resin mix before pouring into the mold. Other materials than limestone are sometimes used to get 'cultured onyx' and 'cultured granite.' The resulting products are different in appearance and are a little more expensive.

The ICPA

The International Cast Polymer Association (ICPA), formerly the Cultured Marble Institute (CMI), is the trade organization for the cast polymer industry. A serious problem has been the inconsistency in quality and performance of cultured marble, particularly in relation to the gel coat. Poorly made cultured marble, particularly for applications that hold water such as basins, tubs, and shower pans, gave the product a bad reputation which hurt the industry. To get control of this, CMI and the National Association of Home Builders instituted a testing and certification program to ensure that products with the NAHB-RC/CMI certification label met the high quality that should be present in a good product. By 1994 this certification label should be present on all cultured marble made by ICPA members. Look for it; it is your assurance that you are getting a high quality product.

Gel Coats

When the mixture of resin and limestone is poured into the mold, the mold is vibrated to cause air in the mixture to rise to the surface (the back of the countertop). The technique, however, doesn't rid the material of tiny air pockets which, when the mixture hardens, would leave tiny pits on the top surface of the counter. This problem is solved by coating the surface with a 'gel' which is a hard plastic sprayed onto the mold and allowed to set before the limestone-resin mixture is added. The gel coat is about .020 or $\frac{1}{50}$ of an inch thick and has a hardness which is between laminate and tile. A characteristic of this surface is that a scratch more than the thickness of the coat cannot be removed because buffing the material takes off the gel coat. Thus, while the basic material is the same all the way through, the presence of the gel coat gives it some of the disadvantages of a laminate in that repair of a damaged surface is usually not feasible.

Costs

Like tile, cultured marble is more expensive than laminate for counters. Its special gel-coat surface is harder than laminate but is still subject to scratching, wear, and knife cuts. This, plus its significantly higher cost, is why it's not usually found in kitchens.

For vanity countertops in baths, cultured marble is about the same price as tile. It has two advantages over tile; it has no grout to absorb water and stain and its smooth surface is easier to keep clean.

Appearance

Cultured marble may be a single color but it can be made with a marbleized appearance that many people find elegant. A well-done cultured marble shower or tub surround, for example, can be handsome.

Minor scratches in surfaces can be polished out by someone experienced in handling the material. Major damage to gel-coated cultured marble can also be repaired but the know-how to do this is not widespread.

When seams are required, the two pieces cannot directly abut one another because there will be inevitable small differences in thickness and these cannot be smoothed out because the gel coat is so thin. Thus seams always involve a mastic which is usually quite evident. For the same reason, gel-coated material isn't seamed directly with other materials.

- In many California models with cultured marble vanities in the guest or hall bath, the builders have again forgotten the home user. In an effort to improve the appearance of the bathrooms, the countertop is extended out over the top of the adjacent toilet tank. It looks nice and adds a little counter space. But it makes it impossible to do anything inside of the toilet tank. Usually this won't be a problem for a few years until a valve needs replacing. Then it will be necessary to move the whole toilet to be able to get inside of the tank. This turns what should be a small chore for the home user into a major job where a plumber will be needed to reseat the toilet. Caveat Emptor.

Nice counter, but it blocks access to the toilet tank.

Cultured-marble countertops are commonly made with the backsplash and the front face all molded in one piece. A small lip on the front of the countertop keeps water from running onto the floor. The ends for the top are separate pieces which are installed at the same time as the top. The material is quite heavy and there is a limit to the practical size of a single piece of cultured marble.

Basins

In bathroom vanities, basins can be put on cultured-marble counters in three ways:

1. The basins are an integral part of the counter.

2. Porcelainized basins are dropped into holes in the counter.

3. Porcelainized basins are mounted under the counter.

Integral Basins—Basins which are an integral part of the countertop are molded of cultured marble and formed at the same time as the countertop. One potential problem with the integral molded basins is that cracks may appear in the basins. These are usually the result of heating and cooling over a period of time. These cracks, if they ever happen, may not appear for months or even years. If they do occur, the basin can be cut out and a standard basin dropped into the countertop. As discussed above, the cultured marble trade association has instituted a testing program intended to significantly reduce the probability of failures of this type.

Basins can be integral with a cultured marble countertop.

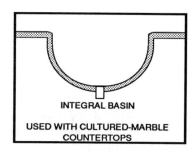

INTEGRAL BASIN

USED WITH CULTURED-MARBLE
COUNTERTOPS

Top-Mounted Basins—Countertops can be molded with holes in them (or the holes can be cut in them) and ordinary porcelainized basins dropped in from the top. This results in the rims of the basins being above the countertop.

Drop-in basins can be used with any countertop

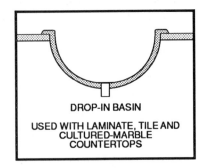

DROP-IN BASIN

USED WITH LAMINATE, TILE AND
CULTURED-MARBLE
COUNTERTOPS

Recessed Basins—The countertops can b e made with holes molded in them with the edges of the countertop around the holes being finished (gel-coated). Mounting tabs are molded into the countertop by the plumber after the counter has been installed. This arrangement has no basin rim or lip on the top.

An advantage to having the basins separate from the countertop is that basins can be replaced without replacing the counter. Disadvantages are that separate basins will be a little more expensive and they don't have the same unified appearance as the integral basins.

In the usual case the basins are a little larger than the hole in the counter so that the edge of the counter sticks out over the basin.

Basins mounted under the counter are possible with cultured-marble and solid-surface counters.

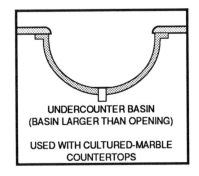

UNDERCOUNTER BASIN
(BASIN LARGER THAN OPENING)

USED WITH CULTURED-MARBLE
COUNTERTOPS

A more sophisticated version is to have the holes that are molded in the countertop contoured to the exact size of the basin underneath. This gives a very clean, smooth, and unified appearance to the counter and basins. This appearance is enhanced even more when the colors used in the counter are matched to the basin underneath.

An improved under-the-counter basin mounting.

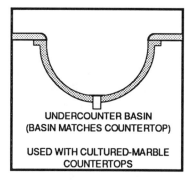

UNDERCOUNTER BASIN
(BASIN MATCHES COUNTERTOP)

USED WITH CULTURED-MARBLE
COUNTERTOPS

Solid Surface Materials

There are a number of different countertop materials falling in the solid-surface category. Corian is the best known but there are many more. They are two to three times more expensive than tile or cultured marble. Solid-surface countertops have a smooth surface which is almost impervious. It doesn't have grout to keep clean or a surface coat that can be damaged. Properly-made seams are virtually invisible. Sinks of the same material are available that can be mounted under the countertop so that they seem all one piece.

Solid-surface materials don't use gel coats; they are the same material throughout. By using vacuum casting techniques the problems with minuscule air bubbles are eliminated. The fillers are harder and denser that those used to make cultured marble. The resin may be polyester or acrylic or a combination of both, giving somewhat different properties to the resulting materials. Corian uses an all-acrylic resin.

Maintenance

Durability is excellent. Burns can be polished out as can cuts or scratches. Because it's the same material throughout, the term "solid surface" is used to describe it and to differentiate it from cultured marble with its gel-coat. These counters can be used anywhere in a home, but the usual place is in the kitchen.

Some solid-surface counters come in a matte surface while others may be glossy. Glossy surfaces will show minor scratches more than matte finishes, but these can be buffed out.

Uses

Because the material can be buffed smooth, two pieces can be directly abutted to make invisible seams. It can also be seamed with other materials such as wood, brass, etc. It is this same property that makes it possible to cut out damaged material and replace it without the repair being visible. Because of the absence of the gel coat and the density of the solid surface material, it's the material of choice for kitchen countertops and any other application that requires a tough smooth surface which is visually appealing.

The primary drawback to solid-surface countertops is the price, but if you can afford them, they're both elegant and utilitarian. They are used in kitchens where their greater resistance to cuts and scratches and their repairability make them more attractive than other materials. In bathroom counters, however, this extra ruggedness is not needed and something less expensive is fine.

Unlike cultured marble, which is cast in local shops, solid surface materials are shipped by the manufacturer, usually in flat sheets, to the local shops for fabrication. The extensive seaming, cutting, and grinding operations needed to put bullnoses and rounded edges on the counters are done in a local shop.

Sinks can be made of the same material as the countertop. When they are mounted under the counter (with an appropriate hole in the top, of course) there is always a concern about how the sink can be replaced if it's ever damaged. The best technique is to make the frame that holds the sink in such a way that the sink can be removed from the under side of the counter. This is readily done in bathrooms with their smaller basins but kitchen sinks are frequently heavy and harder to handle. Some forethought on the part of the cabinetmaker, the plumber, and/or the countertop installer avoids any serious problems if a sink ever needs replacing.

More and more companies are getting into the manufacture of these materials. This will give a greater choice of materials and result in more competition for the upper-end countertop market. Hopefully, this will then give us products at prices that are more competitive with cultured marble and tile.

Ceiling Fans

Ceiling fans come in a wide range of designs and prices. If you have to make a decision about buying one, you'll need to do some shopping. And here are some things to think about when that fan is installed in your house.

Most fans drop down from the ceiling to get the blades closer to the people they are to cool. But we don't always want them dropped down. For rooms with low ceilings (8 feet and under) there is a special kind of fan in which the housing for the fan motor is mounted snugly against the ceiling. Such fans are known as "huggers."

Ceiling fans come with and without light kits. If not included initially, most fans are manufactured so that lights can be added readily. A pull chain on the fan is used to control the speed of the fan. When lights are present, a second chain turns them on and off.

It's not absolutely necessary to have any wall switches associated with the fan unless it's so high in a room that the control chains can't be reached. However, for your convenience, the usual practice is to have an on-off wall switch for the fan and, if lights are on the fan, to have a separate wall switch for the lights. This requires three-conductor power wiring from the fan to the switches rather than the two conductors needed for the fan alone.

Unthinking builders and electricians will sometimes run only two wires to a single switch that controls the fan and lights at the same time. If the home user wants the fan on without the lights or the other way around, one or both of the chains are used. When the fan is high up in a room with a vaulted ceiling this means getting up on a chair, hardly something you want to do. (An alternative is to put a hook on a long stick which can be used to jockey the pull chains around.)

- Yet, that's exactly what happened to our son in his new house in Sherwood, Oregon. In the family room, the builder had initially planned on having a simple hanging light fixture. But our son had a ceiling fan and the builder agreed to install it. The proper wiring could have been provided but no one bothered. There is now a ceiling fan with a light on it and there are only two wires from the switch to the fan.

Needless to say, when the fan is on, the light is also on and, when someone needs a light, the fan comes on at the same time. Either that or the long stick comes out.

Peculiar to a few localized parts of the Pacific Northwest is a practice of having the fan and light wall switches for a ceiling fan located one over the other, one foot apart! When you walk into a house in Washington or Oregon don't be surprised to see one switch (for the lights) at normal height and then to find another one (for the fan) a foot above. It's a practice so common that no one seems to know how it got started.

While unique, this one-above-the-other switch arrangement is not the lowest priced way to do the wiring for a ceiling fan. There's a cost associated with mounting a separate electrical box, mounting the switch in it, and running the wires. Particularly useful to the home user with a ceiling fan is the ability to change the fan's speed. With a simple wall switch, the speed can only be changed using the fan's pull chain on the unit itself.

Now let's save some money! There are readily available units that have both a fan speed control and a light dimmer that will mount in place of one wall switch! The cost of the unit is lower than it takes to mount separate boxes and switches for the fan and the lights. In other words, it would be less expensive to have a wall-mounted speed control for the fan and dimmer for the lights than to have the two switches mounted a foot apart on the wall. (An important note: don't try to use a light dimmer to control a fan's speed. They are different beasts. You could damage your fan motor.)

At least one manufacturer of ceiling fans has a special control arrangement that permits you to not only turn the fan and lights on and off but also to reverse the fan's direction from a control unit that mounts in place of a single wall switch. Still other fans can be operated remotely using a small hand-held controller.

Whenever it's possible to replace a light fixture in a room with a ceiling fan at a future time, three wires should be brought from the fixture to the light switch instead of two. Also, the mounting box for the fixture should be strong enough for mounting a fan. These should be put in place when the house is built.

Security Issues

More and more thought is going into home security. Burglary has become a common thing in our residential areas. You can do something to cut down on the susceptibility of your home to break ins. The most obvious is an expensive alarm system that includes sensors that trigger whenever there's an unauthorized entry. But there are other small, inexpensive things you or the builder can and should do that will help. These are appropriate even with a central alarm system.

Securing Doors

Dead bolts are put into new houses routinely. They operate by moving a heavy piece of metal (the bolt) from the door through a hole in a metal striker plate fastened to the inside of the door frame. If this plate is not well secured, a hard shove on the door will break the plate loose and the whole door swings wide open. Unless instructed to do otherwise, the carpenter who installs these plates will usually use short screws that extend only into the door frame. He should use much longer screws (2½" minimum) to get all the way into the wall studs behind the frame.

Door hinges should also be mounted with screws that reach into the studs behind the door frame. This isn't usually done. Both the striker plate and the hinge screws will be stronger if the gaps between the frame and the studs are snugly shimmed. To beef up the door installation even more, horizontal blocking should be used between studs on either side of the door. These recommendations are from a report developed by the Portland Police Department and are included in the 1993 Oregon Structural Specialty Code.

You should insist on having these things done right. It doesn't cost much at the time of installation but it virtually eliminates one method of easy access for burglars.

You can and should put in the longer screws if they are not put in the house initially. You cannot do the shimming or blocking that makes them stronger. It's better if the proper installation is done initially.

Glass In and Around the Entry Door

The utilitarian purpose of door sidelights is to provide illumination in the entry hall or foyer during the daylight hours. Decorators, suppliers, and builders have seized on this need to make them a decorative and attractive part of the entry way into the house. Unfortunately they haven't noticed how easy they have made it for burglars to get into our houses.

Beware of glass either in the door itself or in the sidelights beside the door. This feature makes it possible for the burglar to break the glass and reach in and open the door from the inside. You could stop this by using deadbolts that require a key to open from the inside. However, this is dangerous if there's a fire and someone is inside the building. The safest approach is to not put glass where it'll let someone get in the house easily.

This can usually be accomplished for the sidelights without significantly degrading the appearance of the entry. The problem doesn't exist for double doors because the deadbolt can't be reached from any sidelight location. For single entry doors, one of two things can be done (and this should happen at the house design stage). For a single sidelight, either put it on the hinge side of the door or space it far enough away that the deadbolt cannot be reached from the sidelight. For two sidelights, space both of them, or at least the one on the deadbolt side of the door, away from the deadbolt. Note that this approach does something else, too; it leaves a place close to the door for the entry light switches—they don't have to be several feet away on the other side of the sidelights as is the case in many of today's houses.

And don't forget the door itself. Many doors include decorative glass inserts; decorators feel that the more ostentatious the house the fancier the front door needs to be. When these inserts are within easy reach of the deadbolt, the situation is similar to that of close-in sidelights: the door can easily be opened once the glass is broken.

When the glass is higher up on the door it's no longer a means of easy entry.

Steel doors are stronger than wood doors but you have to decide between the richer appearance of the wood door and the practicality of steel.

Garage Sidedoor

When there is a garage sidedoor, the door hinges and the dead bolt striker plate should be mounted with long screws for security reasons as discussed above.

Garage sidedoors with windows are security concerns for two reasons: they let people look into the garage from the outside and they can be broken to get at the locks on the inside of the door. Since the sidedoor is almost never on the street side of the house, someone who is 'casing the joint' or who is breaking the door window is far less likely to be seen than they would breaking the sidelights on the entry door, for example. For these reasons, it is strongly suggested that the sidedoor not have glass. If you feel you really need the light such a window lets in, then put a heavy metal mesh on the window which will prevent someone from reaching their hand through the door after the window is broken.

Garage Door Openers

When you are going to be gone for an extended period, it is a good idea to make your garage doors inoperative. Four ways for doing this are:

- Have a separate wall switch in the garage which turns the power on and off to the openers. This is the most convenient way to control the doors. It needs to be done when the house is wired.

- Have the electrician put the door openers on their own circuit in the circuit-breaker box. Then turn off the breaker to disable the doors. (This assumes the circuit-breaker box is inaccessible from outside the house.)

- Get a cord with a switch in it and put this between the outlet and the power to the openers. Let the cord hang down so the switch is conveniently located.

- Unplug the power to the openers when you are gone. This is the least convenient, particularly when it requires a ladder to reach the plugs.

If You Live in the Puget Sound Area

In at least some areas around the Puget Sound, it is common to not include a deadbolt or any other kind of lock on the door between the garage and the house. While it is true that once someone gets into your garage it is easier to break into the house, a lock on this door will make it more difficult and will make the house more secure. If you find a house that doesn't have a lock on this door, then it's suggested that the builder add one, preferably a dead bolt; either that or plan on doing it yourself once you move in.

Fire Safety

Smoke detectors are a code requirement for safety reasons. These are usually installed in the bedroom wing of the house because of the concern of fires trapping people in their beds. Don't hesitate to install extra detectors in rooms with tall vaulted ceilings. The tendency of heat to rise can make these detectors more effective in some cases than those in bedroom halls.

In California, some jurisdictions (Livermore, for example) have a code requirement to put automatic fire sprinklers in two-story houses. Others have special requirements for houses abutting open areas where grass or other wild fires can be a hazard.

Security Lights

When the house is being built, it's relatively easy to have wiring installed for security lights around your home. Where there are no street lights, it's convenient for guests at night if there is a light with an infrared sensor in front of the house. It's also a way of dissuading unwanted guests.

You can have such lights installed by the builder or simply have the wiring put in place and you mount the lights and sensors at your convenience. A switch is needed someplace that can turn these lights off. This switch would usually be in the garage. An alternative scheme is to have these lights on their own electrical circuit so that they can be turned off from the circuit-breaker box.

An Alarm System

While these and other techniques can be used to make your house more secure, the ultimate solution is a security system. You don't have to have this installed when the house is built, but putting the wiring in place before the wallboard goes up will make it less expensive to add the rest of the system later. If the wiring is installed during construction, it's possible to hide the wires. If you want this done, you will need to discuss it with the builder and with a representative of an alarm company.

Heat Pumps

The term 'heat pump' is used to mean a two-way heat pump rather than the one-way 'pumps' which we know by other names like air conditioner and refrigerator. All of these operate on the same principle. When a gas is condensed, it gives off heat and when it expands it absorbs heat and gets things cold.

It takes energy to compress a gas, like in pumping up a tire. In a refrigerator or air conditioner, there's a pump driven by a motor that compresses the refrigerant, a gas, and this makes the gas hot. There are a set of cooling fins used to dissipate this heat. These fins are under a refrigerator or in the compressor unit of an air conditioner. The compressor with its fins is located out of doors for a house's air conditioner and the fins for a car's air conditioner are located near the radiator where the car's fan can help get rid of the heat.

The compressed gas is then carried where it is to do its cooling and allowed to expand again. Now it needs heat to do this and it gets that heat out of the inside of the refrigerator, the room, or the air that blows into the passenger area of the car. We say that it's colder there because heat has been pumped away.

A heat pump does the same thing except that the direction of moving the heat can be changed. In winter the heat is pumped from outside the house to the inside, warming it up. In summer the pump is turned around and the heat is pumped from inside the house to the outside, making the house cooler in the process (and the outside even warmer).

It takes energy to do this compressing and pumping of the gas. This is the reason the electric bill goes up when the air conditioner is working. When a heat pump is working to heat the house there is always the question of whether it might not be cheaper to simply use the electricity directly as electric heat and forget the heat pump. When the outside air temperature goes down, the heat pump works harder and harder to get heat out of the air. Eventually it takes more energy to do the pumping than the heat pump can deliver to the house. At this point, it becomes necessary to cut in a 'back up' heat source or furnace. This may be electricity or gas.

As with any pump, the amount of heat or energy that can be pumped by a unit depends on how big it is. The bigger the pump, the more heat it can move around. If the outside air temperature is close to the inside air temperature, it doesn't take much energy to keep the house temperature where you want it. On hot days it's difficult to pump more heat outside and a small heat pump simply won't cool the house down like a big unit. During vacations the heat pump may be turned off. The bigger the unit, the quicker it will heat up the house, but not nearly as fast as would a furnace designed to generate a lot of heat quickly.

Heat pumps only make sense when a house is well insulated so that temperature changes inside the house happen slowly even with large differences in outside temperature. Under these conditions the heat pump doesn't have to move a lot of energy in a hurry and a smaller unit works fine.

Besides the heat pump that exchanges the heat in the house with the outside air, a different arrangement has the heat pump exchange the house's heat with the ground. Several feet below the surface, the earth maintains a fairly constant temperature. In the summer, the heat pump puts heat into the ground and takes it back out in the winter. By making this exchange over a large enough underground area, this arrangement can work quite well. The amount of ground necessary to accomplish this is fairly large and a lot of tubing must be dug into the ground. This raises the initial cost of these units, making them noticeably more expensive than a heat pump that exchanges with the outside air.

As with furnaces and air conditioners, the proper size for a heat pump will depend on the geographical area, the size of the house, and how well it is insulated. A local heating and air conditioning company should be able to quickly come up with the necessary size of a unit. As with an air conditioner, there is a pump and set of coils outside the house. There is another set of coils inside where you would normally have a furnace. Valves in the lines between the two sets of coils control whether the unit is to operate as a heater or cooler.

Glossary

This listing is intended to help you understand what you're reading about in this and other books dealing with houses. It is not all-encompassing; many terms builders use are omitted because they're of little interest to the home buyer.

3-way switch—Involves two switches that permit a light or outlet to be turned on or off from either switch. The term "3-way" refers to the three ways which the switches can be set: 1) OFF, 2) ON from switch A, or 3) ON from switch B.

4-way switch—Similar to a 3-way switch except that there are three switches instead of two. The light can be turned on or off from any of the three.

A—Ampere. A measure of electric current, used with a number (15A, for example) to indicate the capacity of a circuit, fuse, or circuit breaker.

ac—In today's houses this usually means the air conditioning unit. It can also mean alternating current to differentiate it from direct current.

all-in-one—Type of mortgage loan that includes the construction loan and the permanent home loan in one package. Used with custom or build-to-order houses.

Amp—(*See* A .)

backfill—Dirt that's pushed back against the house foundation after the house is finished.

backsplash—Area just behind and above a countertop, usually covered to prevent water from splashing on the wallboard.

baseboard—Piece of material used to hide the joint where the floor meets the wall; may be wood, plastic, or rubber.

base molding—Molding used as a baseboard.

batten—Narrow piece of material used on the outside of a house to cover joints in walls.

bearing wall—Wall that supports a ceiling joist, floor joist, or roof. May be an outside wall or an inside partition.

bid out—Refers to the process builders use to estimate the cost of a house before it's built.

board and batten—Siding made up of vertical boards the joints of which are covered with batten slats.

board foot—Amount of lumber in a piece 1" thick by 12" wide by 1 foot long. A piece of 1" × 12" that is 8 feet long has 8 board feet. A 2" × 6" that is 8 feet long also has 8 board feet.

boot—Piece of formed sheet metal used to interconnect a heating/ cooling duct and a register.

BR—Bedroom. Could also mean brick.

branch circuit—Electrical circuit with its own circuit breaker in the service panel.

brick veneer—Brick facing on an exterior wall or fireplace.

building codes—Generic term relating to codes for buildings. (*see* codes.)

building inspector—A government employee who inspects buildings to determine if they are constructed in accord with the local codes.

building official—A government official with the responsibility for generating codes and/or enforcing them. May supervise building inspectors.

bulllnose—The rounded outside edge of a tile counter.

butt—Describes how the ends of two boards or the edges of sheet materials meet so that their ends or edges touch in a continuous line. Also describes the end of a board.

CABO—Council of American Building Officials. (*See* Appendix B.)

can light—An incandescent light in a metal can. The can is flush with the surface in which it is mounted. The light itself may be recessed.

Casablanca fan—(*See* ceiling fan.)

casement window—Windows that hinge in or out for opening.

casing—Trim for a window, door, or opening.

caulking—Refers to the compound used to make joints weatherproof and waterproof or simply to make them smooth.

CC&Rs—Covenants, Conditions, and Restrictions. Appended to deeds. (*See* Appendix A.)

ceiling board—Like wallboard (which *see*) but more rigid so that it won't sag when installed horizontally in a ceiling.

ceiling fan—Large ceiling-mounted fan. Also known as a paddle fan or Casablanca fan. Although Casablanca is the name of one manufacturer of ceiling fans, the name is also used generically.

center mullion—In some cabinets, the vertical piece of wood on the front that divides the opening into two parts.

chase—A boxed-in shaft, usually vertical, through which pass various pipes, drains, ducts, and flues.

chipboard—A board made of wood chips that are glued together under pressure

CI—Cast iron.

clapboard—A siding, usually cedar, made of overlapping horizontal boards. Largely replaced by lap siding.

cleanout—Part of a fireplace from which ashes may be removed from the fireplace.

codes—A group of legal documents that define many building parameters. (*See* Appendix B.)

comps—Comparables; describes the process of comparing the values of different pieces of property. Used by appraisers as a major tool in determining property values.

conduit—A pipe or tube through which wires or smaller pipes can be run.

construction loan—A short-term loan made to a builder to finance the construction of a building. Money is loaned only to cover the builder's costs for materials and labor as it is spent.

cop—Copper, as in copper pipe.

crawl space—Space between the bottom floor of a house and the ground under it.

crown—Piece of molding around the top of a room.

D—Dryer.

deck—1) the flat area around a bath tub, *see* also surround; 2) with post and beam construction, the flat wooden surface on top of the beams; 3) a wooden platform on the exterior of houses used for outdoor living.

diag—Diagonal.

dim—Dimension.

dimensional lumber—Single pieces of lumber that are sawed to standard dimensions as opposed to that which is "manufactured."

direct vent—A type of gas fireplace that vents the burned gas directly to the outside of the house (*See* Appendix E).

dn—Down, as in stairs.

door light—The small vertical window(s) on one or both sides of an entry door.

double-hung—Two-window sash where each window slides up and down.

DR—Dining room.

dry—Dryer.

dry wall—(*See* wallboard).

duct—A pipe, usually metal, used to carry heating or cooling air.

ductless—a kitchen exhaust scheme where the fumes, steam, heat, etc., are run through a charcoal filter and blown back into the room.

duplex outlet—The standard electrical outlet in a home. (Two separate plugs can be plugged in, hence the term "duplex.")

DW—Dishwasher.

eaves—The part of the roof that overhangs the outside wall of a building.

el—Elevation.

elevation—A drawing showing the straight-on exterior view of a building.

empty nester—Refers to an older couple whose children are gone, leaving them with an empty house.

ent—entrance.

entry level—(*See* starter house.)

European-style—Describes a style of cabinet without a face frame, also called "box" cabinets. Also used to describe a particular type of hinge needed for this style of cabinet. The hinge is not visible from outside the cabinet.

exfiltration—Leakage of air from the inside to the outside of a building.

ext—Exterior.

face frame—A term used to identify the ring or frame of wood that goes around the front opening of western- or face-frame style cabinets.

fascia—Board covering ends of the roof rafters.

fenestration—Refers to windows and the way they are arranged in a building.

fl—Floor.

flip switch—Electrical switch that is operated by moving the control up/down rather than pushing or tapping on it (as differentiated from a rocker switch, which *see*.)

footing—The base on which a building's foundation sits.

FP—Fireplace.

gable—Describes a triangular section of a wall that extends up from the level of the eaves to a roof peak. The roof line is straight, not curved or broken.

gar—Garage.

GFCI—Ground-fault circuit-interrupter. (*See* Appendix D.)

grout—A kind of mortar used to fill between tiles, marble, or stone.

gl—Glass. Used on drawings to show sliding glass doors.

glazed—From the verb glaze meaning to fit a window with glass panes. Double glazed is used to describe a window with double panes.

gyp board—(*See* wallboard.)

gyp rock—(*See* wallboard.)

gypsum—A white mineral. (*See* wallboard.)

hardboard—A material made from wood fibers that may be made into sheets or pieces to simulate wood.

heat pump—Part of a heating and air-conditioning (HVAC) system. Pumps heat into or out of the house. (*See* Appendix N.)

hollow-core door—A door whose interior is mostly empty.

hose bibb—An outside faucet to which a hose may be connected.

hugger—A type of ceiling fan that uses a minimum of vertical space. Used with low ceilings.

HVAC—Heating, ventilation, and air conditioning.

ICBO—International Council of Building Officials.

in—Inch or inches.

infiltration—Leakage of air from the outside to the inside of a building.

joist—A horizontal beam supported by a bearing wall. Usually used to support floors and/or ceilings.

kiln-dried lumber—Lumber that has been dried in a kiln or oven. Differentiated from lumber that may be wet when used and then dries after the house has been erected.

kit—Kitchen.

laminate—A plastic surfacing material used on countertops and, rarely, in tub and shower surrounds. Popularly known by the trademarked name Formica.

lap siding—Boards of wood or composite material used horizontally on the outside of houses in which the bottom of one piece is made to overlap the top of the piece below it.

light—(*See* door light.)

lin—Linen closet.

lndry—Laundry.

LR—Living room.

MBR—Master bedroom.

mechanical—Dealing with heating, ventilating, and air conditioning as in "Uniform Mechanical Code" and "mechanical subcontractor." (In some parts of the country, mechanical is used to refer to electrical and plumbing as well as the items covered in the Uniform Mechanical Code.)

Mello-Roos—Refers to special assessments districts in California formed to pay for streets, sewers, etc., in new subdivisions. Can add significantly to the tax bill.

miter—Used to describe how two boards meeting at right angles are cut so that cut ends do not show. Miters are usually 45-degree cuts.

MLS—(*See* multiple listing service.)

molding—Strips of wood, usually decorative, used as trim. May be painted or stained and finished.

moulding—(*See* molding.)

move-up house—The next step above a starter house. A house for a growing family.

multiple listing service—A service provided by the local real estate agents that lists all properties for sale in an area along with many of their more pertinent features.

NAR—National Association of Realtors. (*See* Appendix H.)

NAHB—National Association of Home Builders. (*See* Appendix G.)

no duct—(*See* ductless.)

nosing—The front edge of a stair tread that extends or noses over the riser.

no vent—(*See* ductless.)

NV—No vent. (*See* ductless.)

O—Built-in oven.

OC—(*See* on center.)

on center—Used to specify distance from the center of one piece of material to another. Most frequently used to describe the distance between studs or joists.

OD—Outside dimensions.

orange peel—Refers to a wallboard finish that resembles the texture of an orange peel.

OSHA—The Occupational Safety and Health Administration. A federal agency.

P—Pantry.

paddle fan—(*See* ceiling fan.)

party wall—A wall or fence that sits on a property line and is a common responsibility of both parties or land owners.

particle board—Similar to chipboard except that the pieces are smaller (particles rather than chips). Has a higher density than chipboard.

pass through—An opening in a wall to pass dishes through. Usually between kitchen and breakfast nook or dining room.

pocket door—An interior door that slides into a pocket in a wall.

pitch—May refer to the sticky stuff that exudes from lumber but more likely has to do with the slope or pitch of the roof. A 4/12 pitch, for example, means that there is 4" of vertical rise for each 12" of horizontal run.

plasterboard—(*See* wallboard.)

plate—The bottom or top piece of a wall. Studs sit on the bottom plate and are capped by the top plate. The plate is the same width as the studs.

PWR—Powder room or half-bath (not power).

R—Range, when used in kitchens.

r—Radius.

R-value—Resistance to heat flow. (*see* Appendix B.)

recirculating—*See* ductless. May also refer to a recirculating hot-water system that provides immediate hot water to faucets in the house.

ref—Refrigerator.

riser—The vertical boards between the steps of a stairway.

riser height—The vertical distance from the top of one step of a set of stairs to the top of the next.

rm—Room.

rocker switch—An electrical switch which is operated by tapping the top or bottom of the control plate (as differentiated from a flip switch, which *see*.)

RV pad—A concrete pad specifically intended for storing a recreational vehicle.

sawn lumber—(*See* dimensional lumber.)

sconce—Wall-mounted light fixture.

scr—Screen.

shake—A thick wood split shingle, usually cedar, used for roofs and siding.

sheet rock—(*See* wallboard.)

sidelight—(*See* door light.)

sillcock—(*See* hose bibb.) (This term is seldom used in the west.)

soffit—The underside of eaves. Also used to designate the space between cabinets and the room ceiling. May be closed (boxed-in) or open.

solid-core door—A door whose interior is filled as differentiated from a hollow-core door.

spa—(*See* whirlpool tub.)

spec—A house built on speculation with the expectation of finding a buyer for it. Differentiated from a custom or build-to-order house for a which there is a buyer before building starts.

specs—Specifications.

starter house—A family's first house. Usually small and low-cost.

stor—storage.

studs—The uprights used in walls. Usually 2 × 4s or 2 × 6s. Usually wood in residential construction but may be metal.

stucco—A siding material made with Portland cement that is spread on in several layers over a metallic mesh.

subcontractor—A company or person employed by the builder to do a specialized part of the house construction.

subdivider—A company or person who divides land into lots to sell or on which to build houses. Usually includes streets and utilities in the process.

subfloor—What's under the finished floor. Refers to the rough material laid across the floor joists to support the rest of the floor. Also can refer to the sheathing, plywood, or particle board, used to give a smooth surface for the finish flooring.

surround—Refers to the material that surrounds a bathtub or shower. Tub surrounds may be only the flat area around the tub (the deck) or can also include a facing on the front of the tub as well as a backsplash. Shower surrounds are the walls of the shower stall.

T1-11—A hardboard (Masonite) exterior siding with vertical grooves to simulate boards. Comes in 4' × 8' or 4 × 10' panels.

T111—*(See* T1-11.)

T&G—*(See* tongue and groove.)

TC—*(See* terra cotta.)

terra cotta—A red low-fired tile. Used extensively for roofing in the desert southwest but now being superseded by concrete tile because of concrete's greater strength.

tongue and groove—Lumber with a small groove down one side of each board and a protruding piece (the tongue) that fits into the groove when the boards are installed.

tract—A land development area, typically with models of houses for sale.

tread—The flat part of a stair step.

tread width—The front-to-back width of a stair step exclusive of the nosing.

typ—Typical, as in a typical stud arrangement.

unvented—A type of gas fireplace that doesn't vent the spent gasses outside but dumps them back into the room.

U-value—Used to quantitatively describe the amount of heat a door or window conducts between inside and outside air. (*see* Appendix B.)

vaulted ceiling—Arched ceiling.

visqueen—Polyethylene sheet used to cover the ground in a crawl space.

VT&G—Vertical tongue and groove.

W—Clothes washer.

walk-through—Joint action taken by the buyer and builder at completion of the house to find those items that have not been done properly and need to be fixed by the builder.

wallboard—Strictly speaking, refers to all wall materials that come in sheets including plywood and Masonite hardboard. We use "wallboard" here to mean sheets of compacted gypsum (a mineral) with a paper exterior. This is, by far, the most commonly used wallboard. Also called dry wall, sheet rock, gyp rock, gyp board, gypsum board, plasterboard and probably more.

WC—Water closet or toilet.

western-style—Describes a cabinet with a face frame around its front opening.

whirlpool tub—More popularly known by the trade name Jacuzzi and also called spa. A tub with jets of water flowing into it to give a whirlpool effect.

WR—Washroom.

X—Marks a location.

yd—Yard.

zero lot line—A house has a zero lot line when it is built with one wall on the edge of the lot. This wall is frequently a common wall with the adjacent house.

INDEX

ORDER FORM

Name _____

Address _____

City/State/Zip _____

Phone _____

Enclosed is my check for $18.95 ($16.95 for *BUILD IT RIGHT! How to Put Value and Quality in Your New Home* and $2 for shipping).

DIMI PRESS
3820 Oak Hollow Lane, SE
Salem, OR 97302-4774

Phone 1-800-644-DIMI(3464) for orders
or 1-503-364-7698 for further information
or FAX to 1-503-364-9727

Call toll-free and order now!

OTHER DIMI PRESS PRODUCTS FOR YOU

TAPES are available for ....$9.95 each
> #1-LIVE LONGER, RELAX
> #2-ACTIVE RELAXATION
> #3-CONQUER YOUR SHYNESS
> #4-CONQUER YOUR DEPRESSION
> #5-CONQUER YOUR FEARS
> #6-CONQUER YOUR INSOMNIA
> #7-CONQUER YOUR CANCER
> #8-LAST LONGER, ENJOY SEX MORE
> #9-WEIGHT CONTROL
> #10-STOP SMOKING
> #11-LIVE LONGER, RELAX (female voice)
> #12-ACTIVE RELAXATION (female voice)
> #13-UNWIND WHILE DRIVING
> #14-RELAX AWHILE
> #15-RELAX ON THE BEACH/MEADOW
> #16-HOW TO MEDITATE

TAPE ALBUM has six cassettes and is titled:
> GUIDE TO RELAXATION $49.95

BOOKS:
> FEEL BETTER! LIVE LONGER! RELAX is a manual of re-
> laxation techniques and a history of relaxation...........$9.95

> THE RUNNING INDIANS is a unique account of a fascinat-
> ing Indian tribe $11.95

> KOMODO, THE LIVING DRAGON is the only account of
> the world's largest lizard $10.95

> BLACK GLASS, a hardcover novel about a gay man in the
> Merchant Marine at the time of Vietnam $19.95